Life Ahead

Other Titles by the Author

Education and the Significance of Life
The First and Last Freedom
Krishnamurti's Notebook
Think on These Things
The Book of Life
Total Freedom
Reflections on the Self
Freedom from the Known
The Awakening of Intelligence

Life Ahead

On Learning and the
Search for Meaning

J. Krishnamurti

New World Library
Novato, California

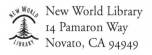 New World Library
14 Pamaron Way
Novato, CA 94949

Krishnamurti Foundation of America, P.O. Box 1560, Ojai, California,
93024; website: www.kfa.org; email: kfa@kfa.org

Originally published in hardcover by Harper & Row in 1963.

Cover design by Mary Ann Casler
Interior design by Tona Pearce Myers

Library of Congress Cataloging-in-Publication Data
Krishnamurti, J. (Jiddu), 1895–1986.
  Life ahead : on learning and the search for meaning / J. Krishnamurti.—
3rd pbk. ed.
      p.   cm.
Includes index.
ISBN 978-1-57731-517-9 (pbk. : alk. paper)
  1. Conduct of life. 2. Sociology. I. Title.
BJ1581.2.K75 2005
181'.4—dc22   2005012961

First New World Library printing, September 2005
ISBN 978-1-57731-517-9

10   9   8   7   6

Contents

Introduction..1

1. What Is the Function of Education?......................23
2. Fear Prevents Initiative...29
3. Authority Destroys Intelligence...................................37
4. Understanding Freedom and Discipline.....................45
5. Learning How to Think..53
6. Is There Such a Thing as Security?............................61
7. Why Are You Ambitious?...73
8. What Is Love?...83
9. The Importance of Understanding Your Mind............93
10. On How to Listen...103
11. Knowledge Is Not Everything....................................113
12. The Quality of Real Affection....................................117
13. Understanding Is Not Memorizing.............................125
14. What Is Envy?..133
15. It Is Understanding That Is Creative, Not Memory....143

16. Understanding the Significance of Words..................153
17. Can the Mind Ever Find Peace?.......................161
18. What Is Life All About?...........................169
19. Living Intelligently................................177
20. Being Educated Rightly...........................187
21. Religion Really Is a Process of Education.................203
22. To Discover the Truth of Things...................217
23. Leaving School......................................227

     Index to Questions..................................231
     Glossary...237
     Index..239
     About the Author....................................247

Introduction

*I*t seems to me that a totally different kind of morality and conduct, and an action that springs from the understanding of the whole process of living, have become an urgent necessity in our world of mounting crises and problems. We try to deal with these issues through political and organizational methods, through economic readjustment and various reforms; but none of these things will ever resolve the complex difficulties of human existence, though they may offer temporary relief. All reforms, however extensive and seemingly lasting, are in themselves merely productive of further confusion and further need of reformation. Without understanding the whole complex being of man, mere reformation will bring about only the confusing demand for further reforms. There is no end to reform; and there is no fundamental solution along these lines.

Political, economic, or social revolutions are not the answer either, for they have produced appalling tyrannies, or the mere transfer of power and authority into the hands of a different group. Such revolutions are not at any time the way out of our confusion and conflict.

I

But there is a revolution which is entirely different and which *must* take place if we are to emerge from the endless series of anxieties, conflicts, and frustrations in which we are caught. This revolution has to begin, not with theory and ideation, which eventually prove worthless, but with a radical transformation in the mind itself. Such a transformation can be brought about only through right education and the total development of the human being. It is a revolution that must take place in the whole of the mind and not merely in thought. Thought, after all, is only a result and not the source. There must be radical transformation in the source and not mere modification of the result. At present we are tinkering with results, with symptoms. We are not bringing about a vital change, uprooting the old ways of thought, freeing the mind from traditions and habits. It is with this vital change we are concerned and only right education can bring it into being.

To inquire and to learn is the function of the mind. By learning I do not mean the mere cultivation of memory or the accumulation of knowledge, but the capacity to think clearly and sanely without illusion, to start from facts and not from beliefs and ideals. There is no learning if thought originates from conclusions. Merely to acquire information or knowledge is not to learn. Learning implies the love of understanding and the love of doing a thing for itself. Learning is possible only when there is no coercion of any kind. And coercion takes many forms, does it not? There is coercion through influence, through attachment or threat, through persuasive encouragement or subtle forms of reward.

Most people think that learning is encouraged through comparison, whereas the contrary is the fact. Comparison brings about frustration and merely encourages envy, which is called competition. Like other forms of persuasion, comparison prevents learning and breeds fear. Ambition also breeds fear. Ambition, whether personal or identified with the collective, is always anti-social. So-called noble ambition in relationship is fundamentally destructive.

It is necessary to encourage the development of a good mind—a mind which is capable of dealing with the many issues of life as a whole, and which does not try to escape from them and so become self-contradictory, frustrated, bitter or cynical. And it is essential for the mind to be aware of its own conditioning, its own motives and pursuits.

Since the development of a good mind is one of our chief concerns, how one teaches becomes very important. There must be a cultivation of the totality of the mind, and not merely the giving of information. In the process of imparting knowledge, the educator has to invite discussion and encourage the students to inquire and to think independently.

Authority, as 'the one who knows', has no place in learning. The educator and the student are both learning through their special relationship with each other; but this does not mean that the educator disregards the orderliness of thought. Orderliness of thought is not brought about by discipline in the form of assertive statements of knowledge; but it comes into being naturally when the educator understands that in cultivating intelligence there must be a sense of freedom. This does not mean freedom to do whatever one likes, or to think in the spirit of mere contradiction. It is the freedom in which the student is being helped to be aware of his own urges and motives, which are revealed to him through his daily thought and action.

A disciplined mind is never a free mind; nor can a mind that has suppressed desire ever be free. It is only through understanding the whole process of desire that the mind can be free. Discipline always limits the mind to a movement within the framework of a particular system of thought or belief, does it not? And such a mind is never free to be intelligent. Discipline brings about submission to authority. It gives the capacity to function within the pattern of a society which demands functional ability, but it does not awaken the intelligence which has its own capacity. The mind that has cultivated nothing but capacity through memory is like the modern electronic computer which, though it functions with astonishing ability and accuracy, is still only a machine. Authority can persuade the mind to think in a particular direction. But being guided to think along certain lines, or in terms of a foregone conclusion, is not to think at all; it is merely to function like a human machine, which breeds thoughtless discontent, bringing with it frustration and other miseries.

We are concerned with the total development of each human being, helping him to realize his own highest and fullest capacity—not some fictitious capacity which the educator has in view as a concept or an ideal. Any spirit of comparison prevents this full flowering of the individual, whether he is to be a scientist or a gardener. The fullest capacity of the gardener is the same as the fullest capacity of the scientist when there is no comparison; but when comparison comes in, then there is the disparagement and the envious reactions which create conflict between man and man. Like sorrow, love is not comparative; it cannot be compared with the greater or the lesser. Sorrow is sorrow, as love is love, whether it be in the rich or in the poor.

The fullest development of every individual creates a society of equals. The present social struggle to bring about equality on the economic or some spiritual level has no meaning at all. Social reforms aimed at establishing equality breed other forms of antisocial activity; but with right education, there is no need to seek equality through social and other reforms, because envy with its comparison of capacities ceases.

We must differentiate here between function and status. Status, with all its emotional and hierarchical prestige, arises only through the comparison of functions as the high and the low. When each individual is flowering to his fullest capacity, there is then no comparison of functions; there is only the expression of capacity as a teacher, or a prime minister, or a gardener, and so status loses its sting of envy.

Functional or technical capacity is now recognized through having a degree after one's name; but if we are truly concerned with the total development of the human being, our approach is entirely different. An individual who has the capacity may take a degree and add letters after his name, or he may not, as he pleases. But he will know for himself his own deep capabilities, which will not be framed by a degree, and their expression will not bring about that self-centered confidence which mere technical capacity usually breeds. Such confidence is comparative and therefore antisocial. Comparison may exist for utilitarian purpose; but it is not for the educator to compare the capacities of his students and give greater or lesser evaluation.

Since we are concerned with the total development of the individual, the student may not be allowed in the beginning to choose his own subjects, because his choice is likely to be based on passing moods and prejudices, or on finding the easiest thing to do; or he may choose according to the immediate demands of a particular need. But if he is helped to discover by himself and cultivate his innate capacities, then he will naturally choose, not the easiest subjects, but those through which he can express his capacities to the fullest and highest extent. If the student is helped from the very beginning to look at life as a whole, with all its psychological, intellectual, and emotional problems, he will not be frightened by it.

Intelligence is the capacity to deal with life as a whole; and giving grades or marks to the student does not assure intelligence. On the contrary it degrades human dignity. This comparative evaluation cripples the mind—which does not mean that the teacher must not observe the progress of every student and keep a record of it. Parents, naturally anxious to know the progress of their children, will want a report; but if, unfortunately, they do not understand what the educator is trying to do, the report will become an instrument of coercion to produce the results they desire, and so undo the work of the educator.

Parents should understand the kind of education the school intends to give. Generally they are satisfied to see their children preparing to get a degree of some kind which will assure them of a livelihood. Very few are concerned with more than this. Of course, they wish to see their children happy, but beyond this vague desire very few give any thought to their total development. As most parents desire above all else that their children should have a successful career, they frighten or affectionately bully them into acquiring knowledge, and so the book becomes very important; and with it there is the mere cultivation of memory, the mere repetition without the quality of real thought behind it.

Perhaps the greatest difficulty the educator has to face is the indifference of parents to a wider and deeper education. Most parents are concerned only with the cultivation of some superficial knowledge which will secure their children respectable positions in a corrupt society. So the educator not only has to educate the children in the right way, but also to see to it that the parents do not undo whatever good may have been done at the school. Really the school and the home should be joint centers of right education, and should in no way be opposed to each other, with the parents desiring one thing and the educator doing something entirely different. It is very important that the parents be fully acquainted with what the educator is doing, and be vitally interested in the total development of their children. It is as much the responsibility of the parents to see that this kind of education is carried out, as it is of the teachers, whose burden is already sufficiently heavy. A total development of the child can be brought about only when there is the right relationship between the teacher, the student, and the parents. As the educator cannot yield to the passing fancies or obstinate demands of the parents, it is necessary for them to understand the educator and cooperate with him, and not bring about conflict and confusion in their children.

The child's natural curiosity, the urge to learn exists from the very beginning, and surely this should be intelligently encouraged continually, so that it remains vital and without distortion, and will gradually lead him to the study of a variety of subjects. If this eagerness to learn is encouraged in the child at all times, then his study of mathematics, geography, history, science, or any other subject, will not be a problem to the child or to the educator. Learning is facilitated when there is an atmosphere of happy affection and thoughtful care.

Emotional openness and sensitivity can be cultivated only when the student feels secure in his relationship with his teachers. The feeling of being secure in relationship is a primary need of children. There is a vast difference between the feeling of being secure and the feeling of dependency. Consciously or unconsciously, most educators cultivate the feeling of dependency, and thereby subtly encourage fear—which the parents also do in their own affectionate or aggressive manner. Dependency in the child is brought about by authoritarian or dogmatic assertions on the part of parents and teachers as to what the child must be and do. With dependency there is always the shadow of fear, and this fear compels the child to obey, to conform, to accept without thought the edicts and sanctions of his elders. In this atmosphere of dependency, sensitivity is crushed; but when the child knows and feels that he is secure, his emotional flowering is not thwarted by fear.

This sense of security in the child is not the opposite of insecurity. It is the feeling of being at ease, whether in his own home or at school, the feeling that he can be what he is, without being compelled in any way; that he can climb a tree and not be scolded if he falls. He can have this sense of security only when the parents and the educators are deeply concerned with the total welfare of the child.

It is important in a school that the child should feel at ease, completely secure from the very first day. This first impression is of the highest importance. But if the educator artificially tries by various means to gain the child's confidence and allows him to do what he likes, then the educator is cultivating dependency; he is not giving the child the feeling of being secure, the feeling that he is in a place where there are people who are deeply concerned with his total welfare.

The very first impact of this new relationship based on confidence, which the child may never have had before, will help towards a natural communication, without the young regarding the elders as a threat to be feared. A child who feels secure has his own natural ways of expressing the respect which is essential for learning. This respect is denuded of all authority and fear. When he has a feeling of security, the child's conduct or behavior is not something imposed by an elder, but becomes part of the process of learning. Because he feels secure in his relationship with the teacher, the child will naturally be considerate; and it is only in this atmosphere of security that emotional openness and sensitivity can flower. Being at ease, feeling secure, the child will do what he likes; but in doing what he likes, he will find out what is the right thing to do, and his conduct then will not be due to resistance, or obstinacy, or suppressed feelings, or the mere expression of a momentary urge.

Sensitivity means being sensitive to everything around one —to the plants, the animals, the trees, the skies, the waters of the river, the bird on the wing; and also to the moods of the people around one, and to the stranger who passes by. This sensitivity brings about the quality of uncalculated, unselfish response, which is true morality and conduct. Being sensitive, the child in his conduct will be open and not secretive; therefore a mere suggestion on the part of the teacher will be accepted easily, without resistance or friction.

As we are concerned with the total development of the human being, we must understand his emotional urges, which are very much stronger than intellectual reasoning; we must cultivate emotional capacity and not help to suppress it. When we understand and are therefore capable of dealing with emotional as well as intellectual issues, there will be no sense of fear in approaching them.

For the total development of the human being, solitude as a means of cultivating sensitivity becomes a necessity. One has to know what it is to be alone, what it is to meditate, what it is to die; and the implications of solitude, of meditation, of death, can be known only by seeking them out. These implications cannot be taught; they must be learnt. One can indicate, but learning by what is indicated is not the experiencing of solitude or meditation. To experience what is solitude and what is meditation, one must be in a state of inquiry; only a mind that is in a state of inquiry is capable of learning. But when inquiry is suppressed by previous knowledge, or by the authority and experience of another, then learning becomes mere imitation, and imitation causes a human being to repeat what is learnt without experiencing it.

Teaching is not the mere imparting of information but the cultivation of an inquiring mind. Such a mind will penetrate into the question of what is religion, and not merely accept the established religions with their temples and rituals. The search for God, or truth, or whatever one may like to name it—and not the mere acceptance of belief and dogma—is true religion.

Just as the student cleans his teeth every day, bathes every day, learns new things every day, so also there must be the action of sitting quietly with others or by himself. This solitude cannot be brought about by instruction, or urged by the external authority of tradition, or induced by the influence of those who want to sit quietly but are incapable of being alone. Solitude helps the mind to see itself clearly as in a mirror, and to free itself from the vain endeavor of ambition with all its complexities, fears, and frustrations, which are the outcome of self-centered activity. Solitude gives to the mind a stability, a constancy which is not to be measured in terms of time. Such clarity of mind is character. The lack of character is the state of self-contradiction.

To be sensitive is to love. The word *love* is not love. And love is not to be divided as the love of God and the love of man, nor is it to be measured as the love of the one and of the many. Love gives itself abundantly as a flower gives its perfume; but we are always measuring love in our relationship and thereby destroying it.

Love is not a commodity of the reformer or the social worker; it is not a political instrument with which to create action. When the politician and the reformer speak of love, they are using the word and do not touch the reality of it; for love cannot be employed as a means to an end, whether in the immediate or in the far-off future. Love is of the whole earth and not of a particular field or forest. The love of reality is not encompassed by any religion; and when organized religions use it, it ceases to be. Societies, organized religions, and authoritarian governments, sedulous in their various activities, unknowingly destroy the love that becomes passion in action.

In the total development of the human being through right education, the quality of love must be nourished and sustained from the very beginning. Love is not sentimentality, nor is it devotion. It is as strong as death. Love cannot be bought through knowledge; and a mind that is pursuing knowledge without love is a mind that deals in ruthlessness and aims merely at efficiency.

So the educator must be concerned from the very beginning with this quality of love, which is humility, gentleness, consideration, patience, and courtesy. Modesty and courtesy are innate in the man of right education; he is considerate to all, including the animals and plants, and this is reflected in his behavior and manner of talking.

The emphasis on this quality of love frees the mind from its absorption in its ambition, greed, and acquisitiveness. Does not love have about it a refinement which expresses itself as respect and good taste? Does it not also bring about the purification of the mind, which otherwise has a tendency to strengthen itself in pride? Refinement in behavior is not a self-imposed adjustment or the result of an outward demand; it comes spontaneously with this quality of love. When there is the understanding of love, then sex and all the complications and subtleties of human relationship can be approached with sanity and not with excitement and apprehension.

The educator to whom the total development of the human being is of primary importance must understand the implications of the sexual urge which plays such an important part in our life, and be able from the very beginning to meet the children's natural curiosity without arousing a morbid interest. Merely to impart biological information at the adolescent age may lead to experimental lust if the quality of love is not felt. Love cleanses the mind of evil. Without love and understanding on the part of the educator, merely to separate the boys from the girls, whether by barbed wire or by edicts, only strengthens their curiosity and stimulates that passion which is bound to degenerate into mere satisfaction. So it is important that boys and girls be educated together rightly.

This quality of love must express itself also in doing things with one's hands, such as gardening, carpentry, painting, handicrafts; and through the senses, as seeing the trees, the mountains, the richness of the earth, the poverty that men have created amongst themselves; and in hearing music, the song of the birds, the murmur of running waters.

We are concerned not only with the cultivation of the mind and the awakening of emotional sensitivity, but also with a well-rounded development of the physique, and to this we must give considerable thought. For if the body is not healthy, vital, it will inevitably distort thought and make for insensitivity. This is so obvious that we need not go into it in detail. It is necessary that the body be in excellent health, that it be given the right kind of food and have sufficient sleep. If the senses are not alert, the body will impede the total development of the human being. To have grace of movement and well-balanced control of the muscles, there must be various forms of exercise, dancing, and games. A body that is not kept clean, that is sloppy and does not hold itself in good posture, is not conducive to sensitivity of mind and emotions. The body is not the instrument of the mind, but body, emotions, and mind make up the total human being, and unless they live together harmoniously, conflict is inevitable.

Conflict makes for insensitivity. The mind may dominate the body and suppress the senses, but it thereby makes the body insensitive; and an insensitive body becomes a hindrance to the full flight of the mind. The mortification of the body is definitely *not* conducive to the seeking out of the deeper layers of consciousness; for this is possible only when the mind, the emotions, and the body are not in contradiction with each other, but are integrated and in unison, effortlessly, without being driven by any concept, belief or ideal.

In the cultivation of the mind, our emphasis should not be on concentration, but on attention. Concentration is a process of forcing the mind to narrow down to a point, whereas attention is without frontiers. In that process the mind is always limited by a frontier or boundary, but when our concern is to understand the totality of the mind, mere concentration becomes a hindrance. Attention is limitless, without the frontiers of knowledge. Knowledge comes through concentration, and any extension of knowledge is still within its own frontiers. In the state of attention the mind can and does use knowledge, which of necessity is the result of concentration; but the part is never the whole, and adding together the many parts does not make for the perception of the whole. Knowledge, which is the additive process of concentration, does not bring about the understanding of the immeasurable. The total is never within the brackets of a concentrated mind.

So attention is of primary importance, but it does not come through the effort of concentration. Attention is a state in which the mind is ever learning without a center around which knowledge gathers as accumulated experience. A mind that is concentrated upon itself uses knowledge as a means of its own expansion; and such activity becomes self-contradictory and antisocial.

Learning in the true sense of the word is possible only in that state of attention, in which there is no outer or inner compulsion.

Right thinking can come about only when the mind is not enslaved by tradition and memory. It is attention that allows silence to come upon the mind, which is the opening of the door to creation. That is why attention is of the highest importance.

Knowledge is necessary at the functional level as a means of cultivating the mind, and not as an end in itself. We are concerned, not with the development of just one capacity, such as that of a mathematician, or a scientist, or a musician, but with the total development of the student as a human being.

How is the state of attention to be brought about? It cannot be cultivated through persuasion, comparison, reward, or punishment, all of which are forms of coercion. The elimination of fear is the beginning of attention. Fear must exist as long as there is an urge to be or to become, which is the pursuit of success, with all its frustrations and tortuous contradictions. You can teach concentration, but attention cannot be taught just as you cannot possibly teach freedom from fear; but we can begin to discover the causes that produce fear, and in understanding these causes there is the elimination of fear. So attention arises spontaneously when around the student there is an atmosphere of well-being, when he has the feeling of being secure, of being at ease, and is aware of the disinterested action that comes with love. Love does not compare, and so the envy and torture of 'becoming' cease.

The general discontent which all of us experience, whether young or old, soon finds a way to satisfaction, and thus our minds are put to sleep. Discontent is awakened from time to time through suffering, but the mind again seeks a gratifying solution. In this wheel of dissatisfaction and gratification the mind is caught, and the constant awakening through pain is part of our discontent. Discontent is the way of inquiry, but there can be no inquiry if the mind is tethered to tradition, to ideals. Inquiry is the flame of attention.

By discontent I mean that state in which the mind understands *what is*, the actual, and constantly inquires to discover further. Discontent is a movement to go beyond the limitations of *what is*; and if you find ways and means of smothering or overcoming discontent, then you will accept the limitations of self-centered activity and of the society in which you find yourself.

Discontent is the flame which burns away the dross of satisfaction, but most of us seek to dissipate it in various ways. Our discontent then becomes the pursuit of the 'more', the desire for a bigger house, a better car, and so on, all of which is within the field of envy; and it is envy that sustains such discontent. But I am talking of a discontent in which there is no envy, no greed for the 'more', a discontent that is not sustained by any desire for satisfaction. This discontent is an unpolluted state which exists in each one of us, if it is not deadened through wrong education, through gratifying solutions, through ambition, or through the pursuit of an ideal. When we understand the nature of real discontent, we shall see that attention is part of this burning flame which consumes the pettiness and leaves the mind free of the limitations of self-enclosing pursuits and gratifications.

So attention comes into being only when there is inquiry not based on self-advancement or gratification. This attention must be cultivated in the child, right from the beginning. You will find that when there is love—which expresses itself through humility, courtesy, patience, gentleness—you are already free of the barriers which insensitivity builds; and so you are helping to bring about in the child this state of attention from a very tender age.

Attention is not something to be learnt, but you can help to awaken it in the student by not creating around him that sense of compulsion which produces a self-contradictory existence. Then his attention can be focused at any moment on any given subject, and it will not be the narrow concentration brought about through the compulsive urge of acquisition or achievement.

A generation educated in this manner will be free of acquisitiveness and fear, the psychological inheritance of their parents and of the society in which they are born; and because they are so educated, they will not depend on the inheritance of property. This matter of inheritance destroys real independence and limits intelligence; for it breeds a false sense of security, giving a self-assurance which has no basis and creating a darkness of the mind in which nothing new can flourish. But a generation educated in this totally different manner which we have been considering will create a new society; for they will have the capacity born of that intelligence which is not hedged about by fear.

Since education is the responsibility of the parents as well as of the teachers, we must learn the art of working together, and this is possible only when each one of us perceives what is true. It is perception of the truth that brings us together, and not opinion, belief, or theory. There is a vast difference between the conceptual and the factual. The conceptual may bring us together temporarily, but there will again be separation, if our working together is only a matter of conviction. If the truth is seen by each one of us, there may be disagreement in detail but there will be no urge to separate. It is the foolish who break away over some detail. When the truth is seen by all, the detail can never become an issue over which there is dissension.

Most of us are used to working together along the lines of established authority. We come together to work out a concept, or to advance an ideal, and this requires conviction, persuasion, propaganda, and so on. Such working together for a concept, for an ideal, is totally different from the cooperation which comes from seeing the truth and the necessity of putting that truth into action. Working under the stimulus of authority—whether it be the authority of an ideal, or the authority of a person who represents that ideal—is not real cooperation. A central authority who knows a great deal, or who has a strong personality and is obsessed with certain ideas, may force or subtly persuade others to work with him for what he calls the ideal; but surely this is not the working together of alert and vital individuals. Whereas, when each one of us understands for himself the truth of any issue, then our common understanding of that truth leads to action, and such action is cooperation. He who cooperates because he sees the truth as the truth, the false as the false, and the truth in the false, will also know when *not* to cooperate—which is equally important.

If each one of us realizes the necessity of a fundamental revolution in education and perceives the truth of what we have been considering, then we shall work together without any form of persuasion. Persuasion exists only when someone takes a stand from which he is unwilling to move. When he is merely convinced of an idea or entrenched in an opinion, he brings about opposition, and then he or the other has to be persuaded, influenced, or induced to think differently. Such a situation will never arise when each one of us sees the truth of the matter for himself. But if we do not see the truth and act on the basis of merely verbal conviction or intellectual reasoning, then there is bound to be contention, agreement or disagreement, with all the associated distortion and useless effort.

It is essential that we work together, and it is as if we were building a house. If some of us are building and others are tearing down, the house will obviously never be built. So we must individually be very clear that we really see and understand the necessity of bringing about the kind of education that will produce a new generation capable of dealing with the issues of life as a whole, and not as isolated parts unrelated to the whole.

To be able to work together in this really cooperative way, we must meet often and be alert not to get submerged in detail. Those of us who are seriously dedicated to the bringing about of the right kind of education have the responsibility not only of carrying out in action all that we have understood, but also of helping others to come to this understanding. Teaching is the noblest profession—if it can be called a profession at all. It is an art that requires not just intellectual attainments but infinite patience and love. To be truly educated is to understand our relationship to all things—to money, to property, to people, to nature—in the vast field of our existence.

Beauty is part of this understanding, but beauty is not merely a matter of proportion, form, taste, and behavior. Beauty is that state in which the mind has abandoned the center of self in the passion of simplicity. Simplicity has no end; and there can be simplicity only when there is an austerity which is not the outcome of calculated discipline and self-denial. This austerity is self-abandonment, which love alone can bring about. When we have no love we create a civilization in which beauty of form is sought without the inner vitality and austerity of simple self-abandonment. There is no self-abandonment if there is an immolation of oneself in good works, in ideals, in beliefs. These activities appear to be free of the self, but in reality the self is still working under the cover of different labels. Only the innocent mind can inquire into the unknown. But the calculated innocence which may wear a loincloth or the robe of a monk is not that passion of self-abandonment from which come courtesy, gentleness, humility, patience—the expressions of love.

Most of us know beauty only through that which has been created or put together—the beauty of a human form, or of a temple. We say a tree, or a house, or the widely running river is beautiful. And through comparison we know what ugliness is—

at least we think we do. But is beauty comparable? Is beauty that which has been made evident, manifest? We consider beautiful a particular picture, poem, or face, because we already know what beauty is from what we have been taught, or from what we are familiar with and about which we have formed an opinion. But does not beauty cease with comparison? Is beauty merely a familiarity with the known, or is it a state of being in which there may or may not be the created form?

We are always pursuing beauty and avoiding the ugly, and this seeking of enrichment through the one and avoidance of the other must inevitably breed insensitivity. Surely, to understand or to feel what beauty is, there must be sensitivity to both the so-called beautiful and the so-called ugly. A feeling is not beautiful or ugly, it is just a feeling. But we look at it through our religious and social conditioning and give it a label; we say it is a good feeling or a bad feeling, and so we distort or destroy it. When feeling is not given a label it remains intense, and it is this passionate intensity that is essential to the understanding of that which is neither ugliness nor manifested beauty. What has the greatest importance is sustained feeling, that passion which is not the mere lust of self-gratification; for it is this passion that creates beauty and, not being comparable, it has no opposite.

In seeking to bring about a total development of the human being, we must obviously take into full consideration the unconscious mind as well as the conscious. Merely to educate the conscious mind without understanding the unconscious brings self-contradiction into human lives, with all its frustrations and miseries. The hidden mind is far more vital than the superficial. Most educators are concerned only with giving information or knowledge to the superficial mind, preparing it to acquire a job and adjust itself to society. So the hidden mind is never touched. All that so-called education does is to superimpose a layer of knowledge and technique, and a certain capacity to adjust to environment.

The hidden mind is far more potent than the superficial mind, however well educated and capable of adjustment; and it is not something very mysterious. The hidden or unconscious mind is the repository of racial memories. Religion, superstition, symbol, peculiar traditions of a particular race, the influence of literature both sacred and profane, of aspirations, frustrations, mannerisms, and varieties of food—all these are rooted in the unconscious. The open and secret desires with their motivations, hopes, and fears, their sorrows and pleasures, and the beliefs which are sustained through the urge for security translating itself in various ways—these things also are contained in the hidden mind, which not only has this extraordinary capacity to hold the residual past, but also the capacity to influence the future. Intimations of all this are given to the superficial mind through dreams and in various other ways when it is not wholly occupied with everyday events.

The hidden mind is nothing sacred and nothing to be frightened of, nor does it demand a specialist to expose it to the superficial mind. But because of the hidden mind's enormous potency, the superficial mind cannot deal with it as it would wish. The superficial mind is to a great extent impotent in relation to its own hidden part. However much it may try to dominate, shape, control the hidden, because of its immediate social demands and pursuits, the superficial can only scratch the surface of the hidden; and so there is a cleavage or contradiction between the two. We try to bridge this chasm through discipline, through various practices, sanctions, and so on; but it cannot so be bridged.

The conscious mind is occupied with the immediate, the limited present, whereas the unconscious is under the weight of

centuries, and cannot be stemmed or turned aside by an immediate necessity. The unconscious has the quality of deep time,
and the conscious mind, with its recent culture, cannot deal
with it according to its passing urgencies. To eradicate self-
contradiction, the superficial mind must understand this fact
and be quiescent—which does not mean giving scope to the
innumerable urges of the hidden. When there is no resistance
between the open and the hidden, then the hidden, because it
has the patience of time, will not violate the immediate.

The hidden, unexplored, and un-understood mind, with its
superficial part which has been "educated," comes into contact
with the challenges and demands of the immediate present. The
superficial may respond to the challenge adequately; but because
there is a contradiction between the superficial and the hidden,
any experience of the superficial only increases the conflict
between itself and the hidden. This brings about still further
experience, again widening the chasm between the present and
the past. The superficial mind, experiencing the outer without
understanding the inner, the hidden, only produces deeper and
wider conflict.

Experience does not liberate or enrich the mind, as we
generally think it does. As long as experience strengthens the
experiencer, there must be conflict. In having experiences, a conditioned mind only strengthens its conditioning, and so perpet-
uates contradiction and misery. Only for the mind that is
capable of understanding the total ways of itself can experiencing be a liberating factor.

Once there is perception and understanding of the powers
and capacities of the many layers of the hidden, then the details
can be looked into wisely and intelligently. What is important is
the understanding of the hidden, and not the mere education
of the superficial mind to acquire knowledge, however necessary.

This understanding of the hidden frees the total mind from conflict, and only then is there intelligence.

We must awaken the full capacity of the superficial mind that lives in everyday activity, and also understand the hidden. In understanding the hidden there is a total living in which self-contradiction, with its alternating sorrow and happiness, ceases. It is essential to be acquainted with the hidden mind and aware of its workings; but it is equally important not to be occupied with it or give it undue significance. It is only when the mind understands the superficial and the hidden that it can go beyond its own limitations and discover that bliss which is not of time.

— *J. Krishnamurti*

What Is the Function of Education?

Have you ever thought why you are being educated, why you are learning history, mathematics, geography, or what else? Have you ever thought why you go to schools and colleges? Is it not very important to find out why you are being crammed with information, with knowledge? What is all this so-called education? Your parents send you here, perhaps because they themselves have passed certain examinations and taken various degrees. Have you ever asked yourselves why you are here, and have the teachers asked you why you are here? Do the teachers know why *they* are here? Should you not try to find out what all this struggle is about—this struggle to study, to pass examinations, to live in a certain place away from home and not be frightened, to play games well and so on? Should your teachers not help you to inquire into all this and not merely prepare you to pass examinations?

Boys pass examinations because they know they will have to get a job, they will have to earn a livelihood. Why do girls pass examinations? To be educated in order to get better husbands?

Don't laugh; just think about this. Do your parents send you away to school because you are a nuisance at home? By passing examinations are you going to understand the whole significance of life? Some people are very clever at passing examinations, but this does not necessarily mean that they are intelligent. Others who do not know how to pass examinations may be far more intelligent; they may be more capable with their hands and may think things out more deeply than the person who merely crams in order to pass examinations.

Many boys study merely to get a job, and that is their whole aim in life. But after getting a job, what happens? They get married, they have children—and for the rest of their life they are caught in the machine, are they not? They become clerks or lawyers or policemen; they have an everlasting struggle with their wives, with their children; their life is a constant battle till they die.

And what happens to you girls? You get married—that is your aim, as it is also the concern of your parents to get you married—and then you have children. If you have a little money you are concerned about your saris, and how you look; you are worried about your quarrels with your husband and about what people will say.

Do you see all this? Are you not aware of it in your family, in your neighborhood? Have you noticed how it goes on all the time? Must you not find out what is the meaning of education, why you want to be educated, why your parents want you to be educated, why they make elaborate speeches about what education is supposed to be doing in the world? You may be able to read Bernard Shaw's plays, you may be able to quote Shakespeare or Voltaire or some new philosopher; but if you in yourself are not intelligent, if you are not creative, what is the point of this education?

So, is it not important for the teachers as well as for the students to find out how to be intelligent? Education does not consist in merely being able to read and pass examinations; any clever person can do that. Education consists in cultivating intelligence, does it not? By intelligence I do not mean cunning, or trying to be clever in order to outdo somebody else. Intelligence, surely, is something quite different. There is intelligence when you are not afraid. And when are you afraid? Fear comes when you think of what people may say about you, or what your parents may say; you are afraid of being criticized, of being punished, of failing to pass an examination. When your teacher scolds you, or when you are not popular in your class, in your school, in your surroundings, fear gradually creeps in.

Fear is obviously one of the barriers to intelligence, is it not? And surely it is the very essence of education to help the student—you and me—to be aware of and to understand the causes of fear, so that from childhood onwards he can live free of fear.

Are you aware that you are afraid? You do have fear, do you not? Or are you free of fear? Are you not afraid of your parents, of your teachers, of what people might think? Suppose you did something of which your parents and society disapprove. Would you not be afraid? Suppose you wanted to marry a person not of your own caste or class; would you not be afraid of what people might say? If your future husband did not make the right amount of money, or if he did not have position or prestige, would you not feel ashamed? Would you not be afraid that your friends might not think well of you? And are you not afraid of disease, of death?

Most of us are afraid. Do not say no so quickly. We may not have thought about it; but if we do think about it we will notice that almost everybody in the world, grown-ups as well as children, has some kind of fear gnawing at the heart. And is it not the function of education to help each individual to be free of fear, so that he can be intelligent? That is what we aim at in a school—which means that the teachers themselves must really be free of fear. What is the good of teachers talking about fearlessness if they are themselves afraid of what their neighbors may say, afraid of their wives or their husbands?

If one has fear there can be no initiative in the creative sense of the word. To have initiative in this sense is to do something original—to do it spontaneously, naturally, without being guided, forced, controlled. It is to do something which you love to do. You may often have seen a stone lying in the middle of the road, and a car go bumping over it. Have you ever removed that stone? Or have you ever, when out walking, observed the poor people, the peasants, the villagers, and done something kind— done it spontaneously, naturally, out of your own heart, without waiting to be told what to do?

You see, if you have fear, then all this is shut out of your life; you become insensitive and do not observe what is going on around you. If you have fear, you are bound by tradition, you follow some leader or guru. When you are bound by tradition, when you are afraid of your husband or your wife, you lose your dignity as an individual human being.

So, is it not the function of education to free you from fear, and not merely prepare you to pass certain examinations, however necessary this may be? Essentially, deeply, that should be the vital aim of education and of every teacher: to help you from childhood to be completely free of fear so that when you go out into the world you are an intelligent human being, full of real initiative. Initiative is destroyed when you are merely copying, when you are bound by tradition, following a political leader or a religious swami. To follow anybody is surely detrimental to intelligence. The very process of following creates a sense of fear; and fear shuts out the understanding of life with all its extraordinary complications, with its struggles, its sorrows, its poverty, its riches and beauty—the beauty of the birds, and of the sunset on the water. When you are frightened, you are insensitive to all this.

May I suggest that you ask your teachers to explain to you what we have been talking about? Will you do that? Find out for yourself if the teachers have understood these things—it will help them to help you to be more intelligent, not to be frightened. In matters of this kind we need teachers who are very intelligent—intelligent in the right sense, not just in the sense of having passed the MA or BA examinations. If you are interested, see if you can arrange to have a period during the day in which to discuss and talk about all this with your teachers. Because you are going to grow up, you are going to have husbands, wives, children, and you will have to know what life is all about—life with its struggle to earn a living, with its miseries, with its extraordinary beauty. All this you will have to know and understand; and the school is the place to learn about these things. If the teachers teach you merely mathematics and geography, history and science, that is obviously not enough. The important thing for you is to be alert, to question, to find out, so that your own initiative may be awakened.

2

Fear Prevents Initiative

We have been considering the problem of fear. We saw that most of us are afraid, and that fear prevents initiative because it makes us cling to people and to things as a creeper clings to a tree. We cling to our parents, our husbands, our sons, our daughters, our wives, and to our possessions. That is the outward form of fear. Being inwardly afraid, we dread to stand alone. We may have a great many saris, jewels, or other property; but inwardly, psychologically, we are very poor. The poorer we are inwardly, the more we try to enrich ourselves outwardly by clinging to people, to position, to property.

When we are afraid, we cling not only to outward things, but also to inward things such as tradition. To most old people, and to people who are inwardly insufficient and empty, tradition matters a great deal. Have you noticed this amongst your friends, parents, and teachers? Have you noticed it in yourself? The moment there is fear, inward fear, you try to cover it up with respectability, by following a tradition; and so you lose initiative. Because you have no initiative and are just following, tradition becomes very important—the tradition of what people say, the tradition that has been handed down from the past, the tradition that has no vitality, no zest in life because it is a mere repetition without any meaning.

When one is afraid, there is always a tendency to imitate. Have you noticed that? People who are afraid imitate others; they cling to tradition, to their parents, to their wives, to their brothers, to their husbands. And imitation destroys initiative. You know, when you draw or paint a tree, you do not imitate the tree, you do not copy it exactly as it is, which would be mere photography. To be free to paint a tree, or a flower, or a sunset, you have to feel what it conveys to you, the significance, the meaning of it. This is very important—to try to convey the significance of what you see and not merely copy it, for then you begin to awaken the creative process. And for this there must be a free mind, a mind that is not burdened with tradition, with imitation. But look at your own lives and the lives about you, how traditional, how imitative they are!

You are obliged in some matters to be imitative; as in the clothes you put on, in the books you read, in the language you speak. These are all forms of imitation. But it is necessary to go beyond this level and feel free to think things out for yourself so that you do not thoughtlessly accept what somebody else says, it does not matter *who* it is—a teacher in the school, a parent, or one of the great religious teachers. To think out things for yourself, and not follow, is very important; because following indicates fear, does it not? The moment somebody offers you something you want—paradise, heaven, or a better job—there is fear of not getting it; therefore you begin to accept, to follow. So long as you want something, there is bound to be fear; and fear cripples the mind so that you cannot be free.

Do you know what a free mind is? Have you ever observed

your own mind? It is not free, is it? You are always watching to see what your friends say about you. Your mind is like a house enclosed by a fence or by barbed wire. In that state no new thing can take place. A new thing can happen only when there is no fear. And it is extremely difficult for the mind to be free of fear, because that implies being really free of the desire to imitate, to follow, free of the desire to amass wealth or to conform to a tradition—which does not mean that you do something outrageous.

Freedom of mind comes into being when there is no fear, when the mind has no desire to show off and is not intriguing for position or prestige. Then it has no sense of imitation. And it is important to have such a mind—a mind really free of tradition, which is the habit-forming mechanism of the mind.

Is this all too difficult? I don't think it is as difficult as your geography or mathematics. It is much easier, only you have never thought about it. You spend perhaps ten or fifteen years of your life in school acquiring information, yet you never take time—not a week, not even a day—to think fully, completely about any of these things. That is why it all seems so difficult; but it is not really difficult at all. On the contrary, if you give time to it you can see for yourself how your mind works, how it operates, responds. And it is very important to begin to understand your own mind while you are young, otherwise you will grow up following some tradition which has very little meaning; you will imitate, which is to keep on cultivating fear, and so you will never be free.

Have you noticed here in India how tradition-bound you are? You must marry in a certain way, your parents choose the husband or the wife. You must perform certain rituals; they may have no meaning, but you must perform them. You have leaders whom you must follow. Everything about you, if you have observed it, reflects a way of life in which authority is very well established. There is the authority of the guru, the authority of the political group, the authority of parents and of public opinion. The older the civilization, the greater the weight of tradition with its series of imitations; and being burdened with this weight, your mind is never free. You may talk about political or any other kind of freedom, but you as an individual are never really free to find out for yourself; you are always following— following an ideal, following some guru or teacher, or some absurd superstition.

So, your whole life is hedged in, limited, confined to certain ideas; and deep down within yourself there is fear. How can you think freely if there is fear? That is why it is so important to be conscious of all these things. If you see a snake and know it is venomous you move away, you don't go near it. But you do not know that you are caught in a series of imitations which prevent initiative; you are caught in them unconsciously. But if you begin to be conscious of them, and of how they hold you; if you are aware of the fact that you want to imitate because you are afraid of what people may say, afraid of your parents or your teachers, then you can look at these imitations in which you are caught, you can examine them, you can study them as you study mathematics or any other subject.

Are you conscious, for example, why you treat women differently from men? Why do you treat women contemptuously? At least men often do. Why do you go to a temple, why do you perform rituals, why do you follow a guru?

You see, first you have to be aware of all these things, and then you can go into them, you can question, study them; but if you blindly accept everything because for the last thirty centuries it has been so, then it has no meaning, has it? Surely, what we need in the world is not more imitators, not more leaders and more followers. What we need now are individuals like you and me who are beginning to examine all these problems, not superficially or casually, but more and more deeply so that the mind is free to be creative, free to think, free to love.

Education is a way of discovering our true relationship to things, to other human beings, and to nature. But the mind creates ideas, and these ideas become so strong, so dominant, that they prevent us from looking beyond. As long as there is fear, there is the following of tradition; as long as there is fear, there is imitation. A mind that merely imitates is mechanical, is it not? It is like a machine in its functioning; it is not creative, it does not think out problems. It may bring about certain actions, produce certain results, but it is not creative.

Now, what we all should do—you and I as well as the teachers, the managers, and the authorities—is to go into all these problems together, so that when you leave here you will be mature individuals, capable of thinking things out for yourselves, and will not be dependent on some traditional stupidity. Then you will have the dignity of a human being who is really free. *That* is the whole intent of education—not merely to prepare you to pass certain examinations and then be shunted for the rest of your life into something which you do not love to do, like becoming a lawyer, or a clerk, or a housewife, or a breeding machine. You should insist on having the kind of education that encourages you to think freely without fear, that helps you to inquire, to understand; you should demand it of your teachers. Otherwise life is a waste, is it not? You are "educated," you pass the BA or the MA examinations, you get a job which you dislike but because you have to earn money; you are married and have children—and there you are stuck for the rest of your life. You are miserable, unhappy, quarrelsome; you have nothing to look forward to except more babies, more hunger, more misery.

Do you call *this* the purpose of education? Surely, education should help you to be so keenly intelligent that you do what you love to do, and not get stuck in something stupid which makes you miserable for the rest of your life.

So, while you are young you should awaken within yourself the flame of discontent; you should be in a state of revolution. This is the time to inquire, to discover, to grow; therefore insist that your parents and your teachers educate you properly. Do not be satisfied merely to sit in a classroom and absorb information about this king or that war. Be discontented, go to your teachers and inquire, find out. If they are not intelligent, by inquiring you will help them to be intelligent; and when you leave the school you will be growing into maturity, into real freedom. Then you will continue to learn right through life till you die, and you will be a happy, intelligent human being.

Questioner: How are we to gain the habit of fearlessness?

Krishnamurti: Look at the words you have used. *Habit* implies a movement which is repeated over and over again. If you do something over and over again, does that ensure anything except monotony? Is fearlessness a habit? Surely, fearlessness comes only when you can meet the incidents of life and thrash them out, when you can see them and examine them, but not with a jaded mind that is caught in habit.

If you do things habitually, if you live in habits, then you are merely an imitative machine. Habit is repetition, thoughtlessly doing the same thing over and over again, which is a process of building a wall round yourself. If you have built a wall round yourself through some habit, you are not free of fear, and it is the very living within the wall that makes you afraid. When you have the intelligence to look at everything that happens in life, which means examining every problem, every incident, every thought and emotion, every reaction—only then is there freedom from fear.

3

Authority Destroys Intelligence

We have been talking about fear and how to be rid of it, and we have seen how fear perverts the mind so that it is not free, creative, and is therefore without the enormously important quality of initiative.

I think we should also consider the question of authority. You know what authority is; but do you know how authority comes into being? The government has authority, has it not? There is the authority of the state, of the law, of the policeman and the solider. Your parents and your teachers have a certain authority over you, they make you do what they think you ought to do—go to bed at a certain time, eat the right kind of food, meet the right kind of people. They discipline you, do they not? Why? They say it is for your own good. Is it? We will go into that. But first we must understand how authority arises—authority being coercion, compulsion, the power of one person over another, of the few over the many or the many over the few.

Because you happen to be my father or mother, have you a right over me? What right has anyone to treat another like dirt? What do you think creates authority?

First, obviously, there is the desire on the part of each one of us to find a safe way of behavior; we want to be told what to do. Being confused, worried, and not knowing what to do, we go to a priest, to a teacher, to a parent or to somebody else, seeking a way out of our confusion. Because we think he knows better then we do, we go to the guru, or some learned man, and ask him to tell us what to do. So, it is the desire in us to find a particular way of life, a way of conduct that creates authority, is it not?

Say, for instance, I go to a guru. I go to him because I think he is a great man who knows the truth, who knows God, and who can therefore give me peace. I don't know anything about all this for myself, so I go to him, I prostrate myself, offer him flowers, I give him my devotion. I have the desire to be comforted, to be told what to do, so I create an authority. That authority does not really exist outside of me.

While you are young, the teacher may point out that you do not know. But if he is at all intelligent he will help you to grow to be intelligent also; he will help you to understand your confusion so that you do not seek authority, his own or another.

There is outward authority of the state, of the law, of the police. We create this authority outwardly because we have property which we want to protect. The property is ours and we don't want anyone else to have it, so we create a government which protects what we own. The government becomes our authority; it is our invention, to protect us, to protect our way of life, our system of thought. Gradually, through centuries, we establish a system of law, of authority—the state, the government, the police, the army—to protect 'me' and 'mine'.

There is also the authority of the ideal, which is not outward but inward. When we say, "I must be good, I must not be envious, I must feel brotherly to everybody," we create in our minds the authority of the ideal, do we not? Suppose I am intriguing, stupid, cruel, I want everything for myself, I want power. That is the fact, it is what I actually am. But I think I must be brotherly because religious people have said so, and also because it is convenient, it is profitable to say so; therefore I create brotherhood as an ideal. I am not brotherly, but for various reasons I want to be, so the ideal becomes my authority.

Now, in order to live according to that ideal, I discipline myself. I feel very envious of you because you have a better coat, or a prettier sari, or more titles; therefore I say, "I must not have envious feelings, I must be brotherly." The ideal has become my authority, and according to that ideal I try to live. So what happens? My life becomes a constant battle between what I *am* and what I *should* be. I discipline myself—and the state also disciplines me. Whether it is communist, capitalist, or socialist, the state has ideas as to how I should behave. There are those who say the state is all-important. If I live in such a state and do anything contrary to the official ideology, I am coerced by the state—that is, by the few who control the state.

There are two parts of us, the conscious part and the unconscious part. Do you understand what that means? Suppose you are walking along the road, talking to a friend. Your conscious mind is occupied with your conversation, but there is another part of you which is unconsciously absorbing innumerable impressions—the trees, the leaves, the birds, the sunlight on the water. This impact on the unconscious from outside is going on all the time, though your conscious mind is occupied; and what the unconscious absorbs is much more important than what the conscious absorbs. The conscious mind can absorb comparatively little. You consciously absorb what is taught in school, for example, and that is really not very much. But the unconscious mind is constantly absorbing the interactions between you and the teacher, between you and your friends; all this is going on underground, and this matters much more than the mere absorption of facts on the surface. Similarly, during these talks every morning the unconscious mind is constantly absorbing what is being said, and later on, during the day or the week, you will suddenly remember it. That will have a far greater effect on you than what you listen to consciously.

To come back: we create authority—the authority of the state, of the police, the authority of the ideal, the authority of tradition. You want to do something, but your father says, "Don't do it." You have to obey him, otherwise he will get angry, and you are dependent on him for your food. He controls you through your fear, does he not? Therefore he becomes your authority. Similarly, you are controlled by tradition—you must do this and not that, you must wear your sari in a certain way, you must not look at the boys or at the girls. Tradition tells you what to do; and tradition, after all, is knowledge, is it not? There are books which tell you what to do, the state tells you what to do, your parents tell you what to do, society and religion tell you what to do. And what happens to you? You get crushed, you are just broken. You never think, act, live vitally, for you are afraid of all these things. You say that you must obey, otherwise you will be helpless. Which means what? That you create authority because you are seeking a safe way of conduct, a secure manner of living. The very pursuit of security creates authority, and that is why you become a mere slave, a cog in a machine, living without any capacity to think, to create.

I do not know if you paint. If you do, generally the art teacher tells you how to paint. You see a tree and you copy it.

But to paint is to see the tree and to express on canvas or on paper what you feel about the tree, what it signifies—the movement of the leaves with the whisper of the wind among them. To do that, to catch the movement of light and shade, you must be very sensitive. And how can you be sensitive to anything if you are afraid and are all the time saying, "I must do this, I must do that, otherwise what will people think?" Any sensitivity to what is beautiful is gradually destroyed by authority.

So, the problem arises as to whether a school of this kind should discipline you. See the difficulties which the teachers, if they are true teachers, have to face. You are a naughty girl or boy; if I am a teacher, should I discipline you? If I discipline you, what happens? Being bigger than you are, having more authority and all the rest of it, and because I am paid to do certain things, I force you to obey. In doing so, am I not crippling your mind? Am I not beginning to destroy your intelligence? If I force you to do a thing because I think it is right, am I not making you stupid? And you *like* to be disciplined, to be forced to do things, even though outwardly you may object. It gives you a sense of security. If you were not forced, you think you would be really bad, you would do things which are not right; therefore you say, "Please discipline me, help me to behave rightly."

Now, should I discipline you, or rather help you to understand why you are naughty, why you do this or that? This means, surely, that as a teacher or a parent I must have no sense of authority. I must really want to help you to understand your difficulties, why you are bad, why you run away; I must want you to understand yourself. If I force you, I do not help you. If as a teacher I really want to help you to understand yourself, it means that I can look after only a few boys and girls. I cannot have fifty students in my class. I must have only a few, so that I can pay individual attention to each child. Then I shall not create the authority which coerces you to do something which you will probably do on your own, once you understand yourself.

So, I hope you see how authority destroys intelligence. After all, intelligence can come only when there is freedom—freedom to think, to feel, to observe, to question. But if I compel you, I make you as stupid as I am; and this is generally what happens in a school. The teacher thinks that he knows and that you do not know. But what does the teacher know? Little more than mathematics or geography. He has not solved any vital problems, he has not questioned the enormously important things of life—and he thunders like Jupiter or like a sergeant major!

So, in a school of this kind, it is important that, instead of merely being disciplined to do what you are told, you are helped to understand, to be intelligent and free, for then you will be able to meet all the difficulties of life without fear. This requires a competent teacher, a teacher who is really interested in you, who is not worried about money, about his wife and children; and it is the responsibility of the students as well as of the teachers to create such a state of affairs. Do not just obey, but find out how to think through a problem for yourself. Do not say, "I am doing this thing because my father wants me to," but find out why he wants you to do it, why he thinks one thing is good and something else is bad. Question him, so that you not only awaken your own intelligence, but you help him also to be intelligent.

But what generally happens if you begin to question your father? He disciplines you, does he not? He is preoccupied with his work and he has not the patience, he has not the love to sit down and talk over with you the enormous difficulties of existence, of earning a livelihood, of having a wife or a husband. He does not want to take the time to go into all this; so he pushes you away, or sends you off to school. And in this matter the teacher is like your father, he is like everybody else. But it is the responsibility of the teachers, of your parents, and of all you students, to help to bring about intelligence.

Questioner: How is one to be intelligent?

Krishnamurti: What is implied in this question? You want a method by which to be intelligent—which implies that you know what intelligence is. When you want to go some place, you already know your destination and you only have to ask the way. Similarly, you think you know what intelligence is, and you want a method by which you can be intelligent. Intelligence is the very questioning of the method. Fear destroys intelligence, does it not? Fear prevents you from examining, questioning, inquiring; it prevents you from finding out what is true. Probably you will be intelligent when there is no fear. So you have to inquire into the whole question of fear, and be free of fear; and then there is the possibility of your being intelligent. But if you say, "How am I to be intelligent?" you are merely cultivating a method, and so you become stupid.

Questioner: Everybody knows we are all going to die. Why are we afraid of death?

Krishnamurti: Why are you afraid of death? Is it perhaps because you do not know how to live? If you knew how to live fully, would you be afraid of death? If you loved the trees, the sunset, the birds, the falling leaf; if you were aware of men and women in tears, of poor people, and really felt love in your heart, would you be afraid of death? Would you? Don't be persuaded by me. Let us think about it together. You do not live with joy, you are not happy, you are not vitally sensitive to things; and is that why you ask what is going to happen when you die? Life for you is sorrow, and so you are much more interested in death. You feel that perhaps there will be happiness after death. But that is a tremendous problem, and I do not know if you want to go into it. After all, fear is at the bottom of all this—fear of dying, fear of living, fear of suffering. If you cannot understand what it is that causes fear and be free of it, then it does not matter very much whether you are living or dead.

Questioner: How can we live happily?

Krishnamurti: Do you know when you are living happily? You know when you are suffering, when you have physical pain. When somebody hits you or is angry with you, you know suffering. But do you know when you are happy? Are you conscious of your body when you are healthy? Surely, happiness is a state of which you are unconscious, of which you are not aware. The moment you are aware that you are happy, you cease to be happy, don't you? But most of you suffer; and being conscious of that, you want to escape from suffering into what you call happiness. You want to be consciously happy; and the moment you are consciously happy, happiness is gone. Can you ever say that you are joyous? It is only afterwards, a moment or a week later that you say, "How happy I was, how joyous I have been." In the actual moment you are unconscious of happiness, and that is the beauty of it.

4

Understanding Freedom and Discipline

The problem of discipline is really quite complex, because most of us think that through some form of discipline we shall eventually have freedom. Discipline is the cultivation of resistance, is it not? By resisting, by building a barrier within ourselves against something which we consider wrong, we think we shall be more capable of understanding and of being free to live fully; but that is not a fact, is it? The more you resist or struggle against something, the less you comprehend it. Surely, it is only when there is freedom, real freedom to think, to discover—that you can find out anything.

But freedom obviously cannot exist in a frame. And most of us live in a frame, in a world enclosed by ideas, do we not? For instance, you are told by your parents and your teachers what is right and what is wrong, what is bad and what is beneficial. You know what people say, what the priest says, what tradition says, and what you have learned in school. All this forms a kind of enclosure within which you live; and, living in that enclosure, you say you are free. Are you? Can a man ever be free as long as he lives in a prison?

So, one has to break down the prison walls of tradition, and find out for oneself what is real, what is true. One has to experiment and discover on one's own, and not merely follow somebody, however good, however noble and exciting that person may be, and however happy one may feel in his presence. What has significance is to be able to examine and not just accept all the values created by tradition, all the things that people have said are good, beneficial, worth while. The moment you accept, you begin to conform, to imitate; and conforming, imitating, following can never make one free and happy.

Our elders say that you must be disciplined. Discipline is imposed upon you by yourself, and by others from outside. But what is important is to be free to think, to inquire, so that you begin to find out for yourself. Unfortunately, most people do not want to think, to find out; they have closed minds. To think deeply, to go into things and discover for oneself what is true, is very difficult; it requires alert perception, constant inquiry, and most people have neither the inclination nor the energy for that. They say, "You know better than I do; you are my guru, my teacher, and I shall follow you."

So, it is very important that from the tenderest age you are free to find out, and are not enclosed by a wall of do's and don'ts; for if you are constantly told what to do and what not to do, what will happen to your intelligence? You will be a thoughtless entity who just walks into some career, who is told by his parents whom to marry or not to marry; and that is obviously not the action of intelligence. You may pass your examinations and be very well off, you may have good clothes and plenty of jewels, you may have friends and prestige; but as long as you are bound by tradition, there can be no intelligence.

Surely, intelligence comes into being only when you are free to question, free to think out and discover, so that your mind becomes very active, very alert, and clear. Then you are a fully integrated individual—not a frightened entity who, not knowing what to do, inwardly feels one thing and outwardly conforms to something different.

Intelligence demands that you break away from tradition and live on your own; but you are enclosed by your parents' ideas of what you should do and what you should not do, and by the traditions of society. So there is a conflict going on inwardly, is there not? You are all young, but I don't think you are too young to be aware of this. You want to do something, but your parents and teachers say, "Don't." So there is an inward struggle going on; and as long as you do not resolve that struggle you are going to be caught in conflict, in pain, in sorrow, everlastingly wanting to do something and being prevented from doing it.

If you go into it very carefully you will see that discipline and freedom are contradictory, and that in seeking real freedom there is set going quite a different process which brings its own clarification so that you just do not do certain things.

While you are young it is very important that you be free to find out, and be helped to find out, what you really want to do in life. If you don't find out while you are young, you will never find out, you will never be free and happy individuals. The seed must be sown now, so that you begin now to take the initiative.

On the road you have often passed villagers carrying heavy loads, have you not? What is your feeling about them? Those poor women with torn and dirty clothes, with insufficient food, working day after day for a pittance—do you have any feeling for them? Or are you so frightened, so concerned about yourself, about your examinations, about your looks, about your saris, that you never pay any attention to them? Do you feel you are much better than they, that you belong to a higher class and therefore need have no regard for them? When you see them go by, what do you feel? Don't you want to help them? No? That indicates how you are thinking. Are you so dulled by centuries of tradition, by what your fathers and mothers say, so conscious of belonging to a certain class, that you do not even look at the villagers? Are you actually so blinded that you do not know what is happening around you?

It is fear—fear of what your parents will say, of what the teachers will say, fear of tradition, fear of life—that gradually destroys sensitivity, is it not? Do you know what sensitivity is? To be sensitive is to feel, to receive impressions, to have sympathy for those who are suffering, to have affection, to be aware of the things that are happening around you. When the temple bell is ringing, are you aware of it? Do you listen to the sound? Do you ever see the sunlight on the water? Are you aware of the poor people, the villagers who have been controlled, trodden down for centuries by exploiters? When you see a servant carrying a heavy carpet, do you give him a helping hand?

All this implies sensitivity. But, you see, sensitivity is destroyed when one is disciplined, when one is fearful or concerned with oneself. To be concerned about one's looks, about one's saris, to think about oneself all the time—which most of us do in some form or other—is to be insensitive, for then the mind and heart are enclosed and one loses all appreciation of beauty.

To be really free implies great sensitivity. There is no freedom if you are enclosed by self-interest or by various walls of discipline. As long as your life is a process of imitation there can be no sensitivity, no freedom. It is very important, while you are here, to sow the seed of freedom, which is to awaken intelligence; for with that intelligence you can tackle all the problems of life.

Questioner: Is it practicable for a man to free himself from all sense of fear and at the same time to stay with society?

Krishnamurti: What is society? A set of values, a set of rules, regulations, and traditions, is it not? You see these conditions from outside and you say, "Can I have a practical relationship with all that?" Why not? After all, if you merely fit into that framework of values, are you free? And what do you mean by *practicable*? Do you mean earning a livelihood? There are many things you can do to earn a livelihood; and if you are free, can you not choose what you want to do? Is that not practicable? Or would you consider it practicable to forget your freedom and just fit into the framework, becoming a lawyer, a banker, a merchant, or a road sweeper? Surely, if you are free and have cultivated your intelligence, you will find out what is the best thing for you to do. You will brush aside all traditions and do something which you really love to do, regardless of whether your parents and society approve or disapprove. Because you are free, there is intelligence, and you will do something which is completely your own, you will act as an integrated human being.

Questioner: What is God?

Krishnamurti: How are you going to find out? Are you going to accept somebody else's information? Or are you going to try to discover for yourself what God is? It is easy to ask questions, but to experience the truth requires a great deal of intelligence, a great deal of inquiry and search.

So the first question is, are you going to accept what another says about God? It does not matter *who* it is, Krishna, Buddha or Christ, because they may all be mistaken—and so may your own particular guru be mistaken. Surely, to find out what is true your mind must be free to inquire, which means that it cannot merely accept or believe. I can give you a description of the truth, but it will not be the same thing as your experiencing the truth for yourself. All the sacred books describe what God is, but that description is not God. The word *God* is not God, is it?

To find out what is true you must never accept, you must never be influenced by what the books, the teachers, or anyone else may say. If you are influenced by them, you will find only what they want you to find. And you must know that your own mind can create the image of what it wants; it can imagine God with a beard, or with one eye; it can make him blue or purple. So you have to be aware of your own desires and not be deceived by the projections of your own wants and longings. If you long to see God in a certain form, the image you see will be according to your wishes; and that image will not be God, will it? If you are in sorrow and want to be comforted, or if you feel sentimental and romantic in your religious aspirations, eventually you will create a God who will supply what you want; but it will still not be God.

So, your mind must be completely free, and only then can you find out what is true—not by the acceptance of some superstition, nor by the reading of the so-called sacred books, nor by the following of some guru. Only when you have this freedom, this real freedom from external influences as well as from your own desires and longings so that your mind is very clear—only then is it possible to find out what God is. But if you merely sit down and speculate, then your guess is as good as your guru's, and equally illusory.

Questioner: Can we be aware of our unconscious desires?

Krishnamurti: First of all, are you aware of your conscious desires? Do you know what desire is? Are you aware that usually you do not listen to anyone who is saying something contrary to what you believe? Your desire prevents you from listening. If you desire God, and somebody points out that the God you desire is the outcome of your frustrations and fears, will you listen to him? Of course not. You want one thing, and the truth is something quite different. You limit yourself within your own desires. You are only half-aware of your conscious desires, are you not? And to be aware of the desires that are deeply hidden is much more difficult. To find out what is hidden, to discover what its own motives are, the mind which is seeking must be fairly clear and free. So, first be fully aware of your conscious desires; then, as you become increasingly aware of what is on the surface, you can go deeper and deeper.

Questioner: Why are some people born in poor circumstances, while others are rich and well-to-do?

Krishnamurti: What do *you* think? Instead of asking me and waiting for my answer, why do you not find out what *you* feel about it? Do you think it is some mysterious process which you call karma? In a former life you lived nobly and therefore you are now being rewarded with wealth and position! Is that it? Or, having acted very badly in a former life, you are paying for it in this life!

You see, this is really a very complex problem. Poverty is the fault of society—a society in which the greedy and the cunning exploit and rise to the top. We want the same thing, we also want to climb the ladder and get to the top. And when all of us want to get to the top, what happens? We tread on somebody; and the man who is trodden on, who is destroyed, asks, "Why is life so unfair? You have everything and I have no capacity, I have nothing." As long as we go on climbing the ladder of success, there will always be the sick and the unfed. It is the desire for success that has to be understood, and not why there are the rich and the poor, or why some have talent and others have none. What has to be changed is our own desire to climb, our desire to be great, to be a success. We all aspire to succeed, do we not? *There* lies the fault, and not in karma or any other explanation. The actual fact is that we all want to be at the top—perhaps not right at the top, but at least as high up the ladder as we can climb. As long as there is this drive to be great, to be somebody in the world, we are going to have the rich and the poor, the exploiter and those who are exploited.

Questioner: Is God a man or a woman, or something completely mysterious?

Krishnamurti: I have just answered that question, and I am afraid you did not listen. This country is dominated by men. Suppose I said that God is a lady, what would you do? You would reject it because you are full of the idea that God is a man. So you have to find out for yourself; but to find out, you must be free of all prejudice.

5

Learning How to Think

We have been talking the last three or four times about fear; and as it is one of the fundamental causes of our deterioration, I think we ought to look at it from a different angle, a different point of view.

You know, we are always told what to think and what not to think. Books, teachers, parents, the society around us, all tell us what to think, but they never help us to find out *how* to think. To know *what* to think is comparatively easy, because from early childhood our minds are conditioned by words, by phrases, by established attitudes and prejudices. I do not know if you have noticed how the minds of most older people are fixed; they are set like clay in a mold, and it is very difficult to break through this mold. This molding of the mind is its conditioning.

Here in India you are conditioned to think in a certain way by centuries of tradition; your conditioning has economic, social, and religious causes. In Europe the mind is conditioned in a somewhat different way; and in Russia, since the revolution, the political leaders have set about conditioning the mind in still another way. So, everywhere the mind is being conditioned, not only superficially, consciously, but also deeply. The hidden or unconscious mind is conditioned by the race, by the climate, by unverbalized and unuttered imitations.

Now, the mind cannot be free as long as it remains molded or conditioned. And most people think that you can never free your mind from its conditioning, that it must always be conditioned. They say that you cannot help having certain ways of thinking, certain prejudices, and that there can be no release, no freedom for the mind. Furthermore, the older the civilization, the greater the weight of tradition, of authority, of discipline which burdens the mind. People who belong to an old race, as in India, are more conditioned than those who live in America, for example, where there is more social and economic freedom, and where the people have fairly recently been pioneers.

A conditioned mind is not free because it can never go beyond its own borders, beyond the barriers it has built around itself; that is obvious. And it is very difficult for such a mind to free itself from its conditioning and go beyond, because this conditioning is imposed upon it, not only by society, but by itself. You *like* your conditioning because you dare not go beyond. You are frightened of what your father and mother would say, of what society and the priest would say; therefore you help to create the barriers which hold you. This is the prison in which most of us are caught, and that is why your parents are always telling you—as you in turn will tell *your* children—to do this and not do that.

What does generally happen in a school, especially if you like your teacher? If you like your teacher, you want to follow him, you want to imitate him; therefore the conditioning of your mind becomes more and more rigid, permanent. Say, for instance, you are in a hostel under a teacher who performs his daily religious ritual. You like the show of it, or the beauty of it, so you begin to do it too. In other words, you are being further conditioned; and such conditioning is very effective, because when one is young, one is eager, impressionable, imitative. I do not know if you are creative—probably not, because your parents will not allow you to go outside the wall, they do not want you to look beyond your conditioning. Then, you are married off and fitted into a mold, and there you are stuck for the rest of your life.

While you are young, you are easily conditioned, shaped, forced into a pattern. It is said that if a child—a good, intelligent, alert child—is trained by a priest for only seven years, the child will be so conditioned that for the rest of his life he will continue essentially in the same way. That can happen in a school of this kind, where the teachers themselves are not free of conditioning. They are just like everybody else. They do their rituals, they have their fears, their desire for a guru; and as you are taught by them—and also because you may like a particular teacher, or because you see a beautiful ritual and want to do it too—unconsciously you get caught in imitation.

Why do older people perform rituals? Because their fathers did it before them, and also because it gives them certain feelings, sensations, it makes them inwardly quiet. They chant some prayers, thinking that if they do not do so they might be lost. And the young people copy them, so your imitation begins.

If the teacher himself would question all this ritualism, if he would really think about it—which very few people ever do—if he would use his intelligence to examine it without prejudice, he would soon find out that it has no meaning. But to investigate and discover the truth of the matter requires a great deal of freedom. If you are already prejudiced in favor of something and then proceed to investigate it, there can obviously be no investigation. You will only strengthen your bias, your prejudice.

So, it is very important for the teachers to set about unconditioning themselves, and also to help the children to be free of conditioning. Knowing the conditioning influence of parents, of tradition, of society, the teacher must encourage the children not thoughtlessly to accept, but to investigate, to question.

If you observe as you grow, you will begin to see how various influences are molding you, how you are not helped to think, but are told *what* to think. Ultimately, if you do not revolt against this process, you become like an automatic machine, functioning without creativity, without much original thought.

You are all afraid that if you do not fit into society, you will be unable to earn a livelihood. If your father is a lawyer, you think that you also must be a lawyer. If you are a girl, you submit to being married off. So what happens? You start out as a young person with lots of vitality, and enthusiasm, but all this is gradually destroyed by the conditioning influence of your parents and teachers with their prejudices, fears, and superstitions. You leave school and go out into the world filled with information, but you have lost the vitality to inquire, the vitality to revolt against the traditional stupidities of society.

You sit here listening to all this—and what is going to happen when you have finally passed your BA or MA examinations? You know very well what is going to happen. Unless you are in revolt, you will be just like the rest of the world because you dare not be otherwise. You will be so conditioned, so molded, that you will be afraid to strike out on your own. Your husband will control you, or your wife will control you, and society will tell you what you must do; so, generation after generation, imitation goes on. There is no real initiative, there is no freedom, there is no happiness; there is nothing but slow death. What is the point of being educated, of learning to read and write, if you are just going to carry on like a machine? But that is what your parents want, and it is what the world wants. The world does not want you to think, it does not want you to be free to find out, because then you would be a dangerous citizen, you would not fit into the established pattern. A free human being can never feel that he belongs to any particular country, class, or type of thinking. Freedom means freedom at every level, right through, and to think only along a particular line is not freedom.

So, while you are young it is very important to be free, not only at the conscious level, but also deep inside. This means that you must be watchful of yourself, more and more aware of the influences which seek to control or dominate you; it means that you must never thoughtlessly accept, but always question, investigate, and be in revolt.

Questioner: How can we make our minds free when we live in a society full of tradition?

Krishnamurti: First you must have the urge, the demand to be free. It is like the longing of the bird to fly, or of the waters of the river to flow. Have you this urge to be free? If you have, then what will happen? Your parents and society try to force you into a mold. Can you resist them? You will find it difficult, because you are afraid. You are afraid of not getting a job, of not finding the right husband or the right wife; you are afraid you will starve, or that people will talk about you. Though you want to be free, you are afraid, so you are not going to resist. Your fear of what people may say, or of what your parents may do, blocks you, and so you are forced into the mold.

Now, can you say, "I want to know, and I do not mind starving. Whatever happens, I am going to battle against the barriers of this rotten society, because I want to be free to find out"? Can you say that? When you are frightened, can you withstand all these barriers, all these impositions?

So, it is very important from the tenderest age to help the child to see the implications of fear, and be free of it. The moment you are frightened, there is an end to freedom.

Questioner: Since we have been brought up in a society based on fear, how is it possible for us to be free of fear?

Krishnamurti: Are you aware that you are frightened? If you are, how are you going to be free of fear? You and I have to find out, so do think it out with me.

When you are conscious that you are frightened, what do you actually do? You run away from it, don't you? You pick up a book, or go out for a walk; you try to forget it. You are afraid of your parents, of society; you are conscious of that fear, and you do not know how to resolve it. You are really frightened even to look at it, so you run away from it in various directions. That is why you keep on studying and passing examinations till the last moment, when you have to face the inevitable and act.

You continually try to escape from your problem, but that will not help you to resolve it. You have to face it. Now, can you look at your fear? If you want to examine a bird, observe the shape of its wings, its legs, its beak, you must go very close to it, must you not? Similarly, if you are afraid, you must look very closely at your fear. When you run away from it you only increase fear.

Say, for instance, you want to give your life to something which you really love, but your parents tell you that you must not do it and threaten you with something terrible if you do. They say they will not give you any money, and you are frightened. You are so frightened that you dare not even look at your fear. So you give way, and fear continues.

Questioner: What is real freedom, and how is one to acquire it?

Krishnamurti: Real freedom is not something to be acquired, it is the outcome of intelligence. You cannot go out and buy freedom in the market. You cannot get it by reading a book, or by listening to someone talk. Freedom comes with intelligence.

But what is intelligence? Can there be intelligence when there is fear, or when the mind is conditioned? When your mind is prejudiced, or when you think you are a marvelous human being, or when you are very ambitious and want to climb the ladder of success, worldly or spiritual, can there be intelligence? When you are concerned about yourself, when you follow or worship somebody, can there be intelligence? Surely, intelligence comes when you understand and break away from all this stupidity. So you have to set about it; and the first thing is to be aware that your mind is not free. You have to observe how your mind is bound by all these things, and then there is the beginning of intelligence, which brings freedom. You have to find the answer for yourself. What is the use of someone else being free when you are not, or of someone else having food when you are hungry?

To be creative, which is to have real initiative, there must be freedom; and for freedom there must be intelligence. So you have to inquire and find out what is preventing intelligence. You have to investigate life, you have to question social values, everything, and not accept anything because you are frightened.

6

Is There Such a Thing as Security?

Perhaps we can approach the problem of fear from still another angle. Fear does extraordinary things to most of us. It creates all kinds of illusions and problems. Until we go into it very deeply and really understand it, fear will always distort our actions. Fear twists our ideas and makes crooked the way of our life; it creates barriers between people, and it certainly destroys love. So the more we go into fear, the more we understand and are really free of it, the greater will be our contact with all that is around us. At present our vital contacts with life are very few, are they not? But if we can free ourselves of fear we shall have wide contacts, deep understanding, real sympathy, loving consideration, and great will be the extension of our horizon. So let us see if we can talk about fear from a different point of view.

I wonder if you have noticed that most of us want some kind of psychological safety. We want security, somebody on whom to lean. As a small child holds on to the mother's hand, so we want something to cling to; we want somebody to love us. Without a sense of security, without a mental safeguard, we feel lost, do we not? We are used to leaning on others, looking to others to guide and help us, and without this support we feel confused, afraid, we do not know what to think, how to act. The moment we are left to ourselves, we feel lonely, insecure, uncertain. From this arises fear, does it not?

So we want something to give us a sense of certainty, and we have safeguards of many different kinds. We have inward as well as outward protections. When we close the windows and doors of our house and stay inside, we feel very secure, we feel safe, unmolested. But life is not like that. Life is constantly knocking at our door, trying to push open our windows so that we may see more; and if out of fear we lock the doors, bolt all the windows, the knocking only grows louder. The closer we cling to security in any form, the more life comes and pushes us. The more we are afraid and enclose ourselves, the greater is our suffering, because life won't leave us alone. We want to be secure but life says we cannot be; and so our struggle begins. We seek security in society, in tradition, in our relationship with our fathers and mothers, with our wives or husbands; but life always breaks through the walls of our security.

We also seek security or comfort in ideas, do we not? Have you observed how ideas come into being and how the mind clings to them? You have an idea of something beautiful you saw when you were out for a walk, and your mind goes back to that idea, that memory. You read a book and you get an idea to which you cling. So you must see how ideas arise, and how they become a means of inward comfort, security, something to which the mind clings.

Have you ever thought about this question of ideas? If you have an idea and I have an idea, and each of us thinks that his own idea is better than the other's, we struggle, don't we? I try to convince you, and you try to convince me. The whole world is built on ideas and the conflict between them; and if you go into it, you will find that merely clinging to an idea has no meaning. But have you noticed how your father, your mother, your teachers, your aunts and uncles all cling hard to what they think?

Now, how does an idea come into being? How do you get an idea? When you have the idea of going out for a walk, for example, how does it arise? It is very interesting to find out. If you observe you will see how an idea of that kind arises, and how your mind clings to it, pushing everything else aside. The idea of going out for a walk is a response to a sensation, is it not? You have gone out for a walk before and it has left a pleasurable feeling or sensation; you want to do it again, so the idea is created and then put into action. When you see a beautiful car, there is a sensation, is there not? The sensation comes from the very looking at the car. The seeing creates the sensation. From the sensation there is born the idea, "I want that car, it is my car," and the idea then becomes very dominant.

We seek security in outward possessions and relationships, and also in inward ideas or beliefs. I believe in God, in rituals, I believe that I should be married in a certain way, I believe in reincarnation, in life after death, and so on. These beliefs are all created by my desires, by my prejudices, and to these beliefs I cling. I have external securities, outside the skin as it were, and also inward securities; remove or question them, and I am afraid; I will push you away, I will battle with you if you threaten my security.

Now, is there any such thing as security? Do you understand? We have ideas about security. We may feel safe with our parents, or in a particular job. The way we think, the way of our life, the way we look at things—with all this we may feel satisfied. Most of us are very content to be enclosed in safe ideas. But can we ever be safe, can we ever be secure, however many outward or inward safeguards we may have? Outwardly, one's bank may fail tomorrow, one's father or mother may die, there may be a revolution. But is there any safety in ideas? We like to think we are safe in our ideas, in our beliefs, in our prejudices; but are we? They are walls which are not real; they are merely our conceptions, our sensations. We like to believe there is a God who is looking after us, or that we are going to be reborn richer, more noble than we are now. That may be, or it may not be. So we can see for ourselves, if we look into both the outward and the inward securities, that there is no safety in life at all.

If you ask the refugees from Pakistan or from Eastern Europe, they will certainly tell you that there is no outward security. But they feel there is security inwardly, and they cling to that idea. You may lose your outward security, but you are then all the more eager to build your security inwardly, and you do not want to let it go. This implies greater fear.

If tomorrow, or in a few years' time, your parents tell you whom they want you to marry, will you be frightened? Of course not, because you have been brought up to do exactly as you are told; you have been taught by your parents, by the guru, by the priest to think along certain lines, to act in a certain manner, to hold certain beliefs. But if you were asked to decide for yourself, would you not be completely at a loss? If your parents told you to marry whom you like, you would shiver, wouldn't you? Having been thoroughly conditioned by tradition, by fears, you don't want to be left to decide things for yourself. In being left alone there is danger, and you never want to be left alone. You never want to think out anything for yourself. You never want to go out for a walk by yourself. You all want to be doing something like active ants. You are afraid to think out any problem, to face any of life's demands; and being frightened, you do chaotic and absurd things. Like a man with a begging bowl, you thoughtlessly accept whatever is offered.

Seeing all this, a really thoughtful person begins to free him-self from every kind of security, inward or outward. This is extremely difficult, because it means that you are alone—alone in the sense that you are not dependent. The moment you depend, there is fear; and where there is fear, there is no love. When you love, you are not lonely. The sense of loneliness arises only when you are frightened of being alone and of not know-ing what to do. When you are controlled by ideas, isolated by beliefs, then fear is inevitable; and when you are afraid, you are completely blind.

So, the teachers and the parents together have to solve this problem of fear. But unfortunately your parents are afraid of what you might do if you don't get married, or if you don't get a job. They are afraid of your going wrong, or of what people might say, and because of this fear they want to make you do certain things. Their fear is clothed in what they call love. They want to look after you, therefore you must do this or that. But if you go behind the wall of their so-called affection and con-sideration, you will find there is fear for your safety, for your respectability; and you also are afraid because you have de-pended on other people for so long.

That is why it is very important that you should, from the tenderest age, begin to question and break down these feelings of fear so that you are not isolated by them, and are not enclosed in ideas, in traditions, in habits, but are a free human being with creative vitality.

Questioner: Why are we afraid, even though we know that God protects us?

Krishnamurti: That is what you have been told. Your father, your mother, your older brother have all told you that God protects you; it is an idea, to which you cling, and still there is fear. Though you have this idea, this thought, this feeling that God protects you, the fact is that you are afraid. Your fear is the real thing, not your idea that you are going to be protected by God because your parents and your tradition assert that you will be.

Now, what is actually happening? *Are* you being protected? Look at the millions of people who are not protected, who are starving. Look at the villagers who carry heavy burdens, who are hungry, dirty, with torn clothes. Are *they* protected by God?

Because you have more money than others, because you have a certain social position, because your father is an official, or a collector, or a merchant who has cleverly cheated somebody, should you be protected while millions in the world are going without sufficient food, without proper clothing and shelter? You hope that the poor and the starving are going to be protected by the state, by their employers, by society, by God; but they are not going to be protected. Really there is no protection, even though you like to feel that God will protect you. It is just a nice idea to pacify your fear; so you do not question anything, but just believe in God. To start with the idea that you are going to be protected by God has no meaning. But if you really go into this whole problem of fear, then you will find out whether God will protect you or not.

When there is the feeling of affection, there is no fear, no exploitation, and then there is no problem.

Questioner: What is society?

Krishnamurti: What is society? And what is the family? Let us find out, step by step, how society is created, how it comes into being.

What is the family? When you say, "This is my family," what do you mean? Your father, your mother, your brother and sister, the sense of closeness, the fact that you are living together in the same house, the feeling that your parents are going to protect you, the ownership of certain property, of jewels, saris, clothes—all this is the basis of the family. There are other families like yours living in other houses, feeling exactly the same things you feel, having the sense of "my wife," "my husband," "my children," "my house," "my clothes," "my car"; there are many such families living on the same piece of earth, and they come to have the feeling that they must not be invaded by still other families. So they begin to make laws. The powerful families build themselves into high positions, they acquire big properties, they have more money, more clothes, more cars; they get together and frame the laws, they tell the rest of us what to do. So gradually there comes into being a society, with laws, regulations, policemen, with an army and a navy. Ultimately the whole earth becomes populated by societies of various kinds. Then people get antagonistic ideas and want to overthrow those who are established in high positions, who have all the means of power. They break down that particular society and form another.

Society is the relationship between people—the relationship between one person and another, between one family and another, between one group and another, and between the individual and the group. Human relationship is society, the relationship between you and me. If I am very greedy, very cunning, if I have great power and authority, I am going to push you out; and you will try to do the same to me. So we make laws. But others come and break our laws, establishing another set of laws, and this goes on all the time. In society, which is human relationship, there is constant conflict. This is the simple basis of society, which becomes more and more complex as human beings themselves become more and more complex in their ideas, in their wants, in their institutions and their industries.

Questioner: Can you be free while living in this society?

Krishnamurti: If I depend on society for my satisfaction, for my comfort, can I ever be free? If I depend on my father for affection, for money, for the initiative to do things, or if I depend in some way on a guru, I am not free, am I? So, is it possible to be free as long as I am psychologically dependent? Surely, freedom is possible only when I have capacity, initiative, when I can think independently, when I am not afraid of what anybody says, when I really want to find out what is true and am not greedy, envious, jealous. As long as I am envious, greedy, I am psychologically depending on society; and as long as I depend on society in that way, I am not free. But if I cease to be greedy, I am free.

Questioner: Why do people want to live in society when they can live alone?

Krishnamurti: Can you live alone?

Questioner: I live in society because my father and mother live in society.

Krishnamurti: To get a job, to earn a livelihood, have you not to live in society? Can you live alone? For your food, clothing, and shelter you depend on somebody. You cannot live in isolation. No entity is completely alone. It is only in death that you are alone. In living you are always related—related to your father, to your brother, to the beggar, to the road-mender, to the merchant, to the collector. You are always related; and because you do not understand that relationship, there is conflict. But if you understand the relationship between yourself and another, there is no conflict, and then the question of living alone does not arise.

Questioner: Since we are always related to one another, is it not true that we can never be absolutely free?

Krishnamurti: We don't understand what relationship is, right relationship. Suppose I depend on you for my gratification, for my comfort, for my sense of security, how can I ever be free? But if I do not depend in that way, I am still related to you, am I not? I depend on you for some kind of emotional, physical, or intellectual comfort, therefore I am not free. I cling to my parents because I want some kind of safety, which means that my relationship to them is one of dependence and is based on fear. How then can I have any relationship which is free? There is freedom in relationship only when there is no fear. So, to have right relationship, I must set about freeing myself from this psychological dependency which breeds fear.

Questioner: How can we be free when our parents depend on us in their old age?

Krishnamurti: Because they are old, they depend on you to support them. So what happens? They expect you to earn a livelihood that will enable you to clothe and feed them; and if what you want to do is to become a carpenter or an artist, even though you may earn no money at all, they will say that you must not do it because you have to support them. Just think about this. I am not saying it is good or bad. By saying it is good or bad we put an end to thinking. Your parents' demand that you should provide for them prevents you from living your own life, and living your own life is considered selfish; so you become the slave of your parents.

You may say that the state should look after old people through old age pensions and various other means of security. But in a country where there is overpopulation, insufficiency of national income, lack of productivity and so on, the state cannot look after old people. So elderly parents depend on the young, and the young always fit into the groove of tradition and are destroyed. But this is not a problem to be discussed by me. You all have to think about it and work it out.

I naturally want to support my parents within reasonable limits. But suppose I also want to do something which pays very little. Suppose I want to become a religious person and live my life to finding out what God is, what truth is. That way of living may not bring me any money, and if I pursue it I may have to give up my family—which means they will probably starve, like millions of other people. What am I to do? As long as I am afraid of what people will say—that I am not a dutiful son, that I am an unworthy son—I shall never be a creative human being. To be a happy, creative human being, I must have a great deal of initiative.

Questioner: Would it be good on our part to allow our parents to starve?

Krishnamurti: You are not putting it in the right way. Suppose I really want to become an artist, a painter, and I know painting will bring me very little money. What am I to do? Sacrifice my deep urge to paint and become a clerk? That is what generally happens, is it not? I become a clerk, and for the rest of my life I am in great conflict, I am in misery; and because I am suffering, frustrated, I make life miserable for my wife and children. But if, as a young artist, I see the significance of all this, I say to my parents, "I want to paint and I will give you what I can from the little I have; that is all I can do."

You have asked certain questions, and I have answered them. But if you do not really think about these questions, if you do not go into them for yourself more and more deeply and approach them from different angles, look at them in different ways, then you will only say, "This is good and that is bad; this is duty and that is not duty; this is right and that is wrong"— and this will not lead you any further. Whereas, if you and I think about all these questions together, and if you and your parents and teachers discuss them, go into them, then your intelligence will be awakened, and when these problems arise in your daily life you will be able to meet them. But you will not be able to meet them if you merely accept what I am saying. My answers to your questions are only intended to awaken your intelligence, so that you will think out these problems for yourself and thus be capable of meeting life rightly.

7

Why Are You Ambitious?

You know I have been talking about fear; and it is very important for us to be conscious and aware of fear. Do you know how it comes into being? Throughout the world we can see that people are perverted by fear, twisted in their ideas, in their feelings, in their activities. So we ought to go into the problem of fear from every possible angle, not only from the moral and economic viewpoint of society, but also from the point of view of our inward, psychological struggles.

As I have said, fear for outward and inward security twists the mind and distorts our thinking. I hope you have thought a little about this, because the more clearly you consider this and see the truth of it, the freer you will be from all dependence. The older people have not brought about a marvelous society; the parents, the ministers, the teachers, the rulers, the priests have not created a beautiful world. On the contrary, they have created a frightful, brutal world in which everybody is fighting somebody; in which one group is against another, one class against another, one nation against another, one ideology or set of beliefs against another. The world in which you are growing up is an ugly world, a sorrowful world, where the older people try to smother you with their ideas, their beliefs, their ugliness; and if you are merely going to follow the ugly pattern of the older people who have brought about this monstrous society, what is the point of being educated, what is the point of living at all?

If you look around you will see that throughout the world there is appalling destruction and human misery. You may read about wars in history, but you do not know the actuality of it, how cities are completely destroyed, how the hydrogen bomb, when dropped on an island, causes the whole island to disappear. Ships are bombed and they go up into thin air. There is appalling destruction due to this so-called advancement, and it is in such a world you are growing up. You may have a good time while you are young, a happy time; but when you grow older, unless you are very alert, watchful of your thoughts, of your feelings, you will perpetuate this world of battles, of ruthless ambitions, a world where each one is competing with another, where there is misery, starvation, overpopulation, and disease.

So, while you are young, is it not very important for you to be helped by the right kind of teacher to think about all these things, and not just be taught to pass some dull examinations? Life is sorrow, death, love, hate, cruelty, disease, starvation, and you have to begin to consider all these things. That is why I feel it is good that you and I should go into these problems together, so that your intelligence is awakened and you begin to have some real feeling about all these things. Then you will not grow up just to be married off and become a thoughtless clerk or a breeding machine, losing yourself in this ugly pattern of life like waters in the sands.

One of the causes of fear is ambition, is it not? And are you all not ambitious? What is your ambition? To pass some examination?

To become a governor? Or, if you are very young, perhaps you just want to become an engine-driver, to drive engines across a bridge. But why are you ambitious? What does it mean? Have you ever thought about it? Have you noticed older people, how ambitious they are? In your own family, have you not heard your father or your uncle talk about getting more salary, or occupying some prominent position? In our society—and I have explained what our society is, everybody is doing that, trying to be on top. They all want to become somebody, do they not? The clerk wants to become the manager, the manager wants to become something bigger, and so on and so on—the continual struggle to become. If I am a teacher, I want to become the principal; if I am the principal, I want to become the manager. If you are ugly, you want to be beautiful. Or you want to have more money, more saris, more clothes, more furniture, houses, property—more and more and more. Not only outwardly, but also inwardly, in the so-called spiritual sense, you want to become somebody, though you cover that ambition by a lot of words. Have you not noticed this? And you think it is perfectly all right, don't you? You think it is perfectly normal, justifiable, right.

Now, what has ambition done in the world? So few of us have ever thought about it. When you see a man struggling to gain, to achieve, to get ahead of somebody else, have you ever asked yourself what is in his heart? If you will look into your own heart when you are ambitious, when you are struggling to become somebody, spiritually or in the worldly sense, you will find there the worm of fear. The ambitious man is the most frightened of men, because he is afraid to be what he is. He says, "If I remain what I am, I shall be nobody, therefore I must be somebody, I must become a magistrate, a judge, a minister." If you examine this process very closely, if you go behind the screen of words and ideas, beyond the wall of status and success, you will find there is fear; because the ambitious man is afraid to be what he is. He thinks that what he is in himself is insignificant, poor, ugly; he feels lonely, utterly empty, therefore he says, "I must go and achieve something." So either he goes after what he calls God, which is just another form of ambition, or he tries to become somebody in the world. In this way his loneliness, his sense of inward emptiness—of which he is really frightened—is covered up. He runs away from it, and ambition becomes the means through which he can escape.

So, what is happening in the world? Everybody is fighting somebody. One man feels less than another and struggles to get to the top. There is no love, there is no consideration, there is no deep thought. Our society is a constant battle of man against man. This struggle is born of the ambition to become somebody, and the older people encourage you to be ambitious. They want you to amount to something, to marry a rich man or a rich woman, to have influential friends. Being frightened, ugly in their hearts, they try to make you like themselves; and you in turn *want* to be like them, because you see the glamour of it all. When the governor comes, everybody bows down to the earth to receive him, they give him garlands, make speeches. He loves it, and you love it too. You feel honored if you know his uncle or his clerk, and you bask in the sunshine of his ambition, his achievements. So you are easily caught in the ugly web of the older generation, in the pattern of this monstrous society. Only if you are very alert, constantly watchful, only if you are not afraid and do not accept, but question all the time—only then will you not be caught, but go beyond and create a different world.

That is why it is very important for you to find your true vocation. Do you know what *vocation* means? Something which you love to do, which is natural to you. After all, that is the function of education—to help you to grow independently so that you are free of ambition and can find your true vocation. The ambitious man has never found his true vocation; if he had, he would not be ambitious.

So, it is the responsibility of the teachers, of the principal, to help you to be intelligent, unafraid, so that you can find your true vocation, your own way of life, the way you really want to live and earn your livelihood. This implies a revolution in thinking; because, in our present society, the man who can talk, the man who can write, the man who can rule, the man who has a big car is thought to be in a marvelous position; and the man who digs in the garden, who cooks, who builds a house is despised.

Are you aware of your own feelings when you look at a mason, at the man who mends the road, or drives a taxi, or pulls a cart? Have you noticed how you regard him with absolute contempt? To you he hardly even exists. You disregard him; but when a man has a title of some kind, or is a banker, a merchant, a guru, or a minister, you immediately respect him. But if you really find your true vocation, you will help to break down this rotten system completely; because then, whether you are a gardener, or a painter, or an engineer, you will be doing something which you love with your whole being; and that is not ambition. To do something marvelously well, to do it completely, truly, according to what you deeply think and feel—that is not ambition and in that there is no fear.

To help you to discover your true vocation is very difficult, because it means that the teacher has to pay a great deal of attention to each student to find out what he is capable of. He has to help him not to be afraid, but to question, to investigate. You may be a potential writer, or a poet, or a painter. Whatever it is, if you really love to do it, you are not ambitious; because in love there is no ambition.

So, is it not very important while you are young that you should be helped to awaken your own intelligence and thereby find your true vocation? Then you will love what you do, right through life, which means there will be no ambition, no competition, no fighting another for position, for prestige; and then perhaps you will be able to create a new world. In that new world all the ugly things of the older generation will cease to exist—their wars, their mischief, their separative gods, their rituals which mean absolutely nothing, their sovereign governments, their violence. That is why the responsibility of the teachers, and of the students, is very great.

Questioner: If somebody has an ambition to be an engineer, does it not mean that he is interested in engineering?

Krishnamurti: Would you say that being interested in something is ambition? We can give to that word *ambition* various meanings. To me, ambition is the outcome of fear. But if as a boy I am interested in being an engineer because I want to build beautiful structures, marvelous irrigation systems, splendid roads, it means I love engineering; and that is not ambition. In love there is no fear.

So, ambition and interest are two different things, are they not? If I am really interested in painting, if I love to paint, then I do not compete to be the best or the most famous painter. I just love painting. You may be better at painting than I, but I do not compare myself with you. When I paint, I love what I am doing, and for me that is sufficient in itself.

Questioner: What is the easiest way of finding God?

Krishnamurti: I am afraid there is no easy way, because to find God is a most difficult, a most arduous thing. Is not what we call

God something which the mind creates? You know what the mind is. The mind is the result of time, and it can create anything, any illusion. It has the power of creating ideas, of projecting itself in fancies, in imagination; it is constantly accumulating, discarding, choosing. Being prejudiced, narrow, limited, the mind can picture God, it can imagine what God is according to its own limitations. Because certain teachers, priests, and so-called saviors have said there is God and have described him, the mind can imagine God in those terms; but that image is not God. God is something that cannot be found by the mind.

To understand God, you must first understand your own mind—which is very difficult. The mind is very complex, and to understand it is not easy. But it is easy enough to sit down and go into some kind of dream, have various visions, illusions, and then think that you are very near to God. The mind can deceive itself enormously. So, to really experience that which may be called God, you must be completely quiet; and have you not found out how extremely difficult that is? Have you not noticed how even the older people never sit quietly, how they fidget, how they wiggle their toes and move their hands? It is difficult physically to sit still; and how much more difficult it is for the mind to be still! You may follow some guru and force your mind to be quiet; but your mind is not really quiet. It is still restless, like a child that is made to stand in the corner. It is a great art for the mind to be completely silent without coercion; and only then is there a possibility of experiencing that which may be called God.

Questioner: Is God everywhere?

Krishnamurti: Are you really interested to find out? You ask questions, and then subside; you do not listen. Have you noticed how the older people almost never listen to you? They rarely listen to you because they are so enclosed in their own thoughts, in their own emotions, in their own satisfactions and sorrows. I hope you have noticed this. If you know how to observe and how to listen, really listen, you will find out a lot of things, not only about people but about the world.

Here is this boy asking if God is everywhere. He is rather young to be asking that question. He does not know what it really means. He probably has a vague inkling of something—the feeling of beauty, an awareness of the birds in the sky, of running waters, of a nice, smiling face, of a leaf dancing in the wind, of a woman carrying a burden. And there is anger, noise, sorrow—all that is in the air. So he is naturally interested and anxious to find out what life is all about. He hears the older people talking about God, and he is puzzled. It is very important for him to ask such a question, is it not? And it is equally important for you all to seek the answer; because, as I said the other day, you will begin to catch the meaning of all this inwardly, unconsciously, deep down; and then, as you grow up, you will have hints of other things besides this ugly world of struggle. The world is beautiful, the earth is bountiful; but we are the spoilers of it.

Questioner: What is the real goal of life?

Krishnamurti: It is, first of all, what you make of it. It is what you make of life.

Questioner: As far as reality is concerned, it must be something else. I am not particularly interested in having a personal goal, but I want to know what is the goal for everybody.

Krishnamurti: How will you find out? Who will show you? Can you discover it by reading? If you read, one author may give you a particular method, while another author may offer quite a different method. If you go to a man who is suffering, he will say that the goal of life is to be happy. If you go to a man who is starving, who has not had sufficient food for years, his goal will be to have a full tummy. If you go to a politician, his goal will be to become one of the directors, one of the rulers of the world. If you ask a young woman, she will say, "My goal is to have a baby." If you go to a *sannyasi*, his goal is to find God. The goal, the underlying desire of people is generally to find something gratifying, comforting; they want some form of security, safety, so that they will have no doubts, no questions, no anxiety, no fear. Most of us want something permanent to which we can cling, do we not?

So, the general goal of life for man is some kind of hope, some kind of safety, some kind of permanency. Don't say, "Is that all?" That is the immediate fact, and you must first be fully acquainted with that. You must question all that—which means, you must question yourself. The general goal of life for man is embedded in you, because you are part of the whole. You yourself want safety, permanency, happiness; you want something to which to cling.

Now, to find out if there is something else beyond, some truth which is not of the mind, all the illusions of the mind must be finished with; that is, you must understand them and put them aside. Only then can you discover the real thing, whether there is a goal or not. To stipulate that there must be a goal, or to believe that there is a goal, is merely another illusion. But if you can question all your conflicts, struggles, pains, vanities, ambitions, hopes, fears, and go through them, go beyond and above them, then you will find out.

Questioner: If I develop higher influences, will I eventually see the ultimate?

Krishnamurti: How can you see the ultimate as long as there are many barriers between you and that? First you must remove the barriers. You cannot sit in a closed room and know what fresh air is like. To have fresh air you must open the windows. Similarly, you must see all the barriers, all the limitations and conditionings within yourself; you must understand them and put them aside. Then you will find out. But to sit on this side and try to find out what is on the other has no meaning.

8

What Is Love?

As you know, we have been talking a great deal about fear, because it is a very powerful factor in our lives. Let us now talk for a while about love; let us find out whether behind this word and this feeling—which for all of us has so much significance—there is also that peculiar element of apprehension, of anxiety, the thing which grown-up people know as loneliness.

Do you know what love is? Do you love your father, your mother, your brother, your teacher, your friend? Do you know what it means to love? When you say that you love your parents, what does it mean? You feel safe with them, you feel at home with them. Your parents are protecting you, they are giving you money, shelter, food, and clothing, and you feel with them a sense of close relationship, don't you? You also feel that you can trust them—or you may not. Probably you do not talk to them as easily and happily as you do to your own friends. But you respect them, you are guided by them, you obey them, you have a certain sense of responsibility towards them, feeling that you must support them when they are old. They in turn love you, they want to protect you, to guide you, to help you—at least they say so. They want to marry you off so that you will lead a so-called moral life and stay out of trouble, so that you will have a husband to look after you, or a wife to cook for you and bear your children. All this is called love, is it not?

We cannot immediately say what is love, because love is not readily explained by words. It does not come to us easily. Yet without love, life is very barren; without love, the trees, the birds, the smile of men and women, the bridge across the river, the boatmen, and the animals have no meaning. Without love, life is like a shallow pool. In a deep river there is richness and many fish can live; but the shallow pool is soon dried up by the strong sun, and nothing remains except mud and dirt.

For most of us, love is an extraordinarily difficult thing to understand because our lives are very shallow. We want to be loved, and also we want to love, and behind that word there is a lurking fear. So, is it not very important for each one of us to find out what this extraordinary thing really is? And we can find out only if we are aware of how we regard other human beings, how we look at the trees, at the animals, at a stranger, at the man who is hungry. We must be aware of how we regard our friends, of how we regard our guru, if we have one, of how we regard our parents.

When you say, "I love my father and my mother, I love my guardian, my teacher," what does it mean? When you respect somebody tremendously and look up to them, when you feel it is your duty to obey them and they in turn expect your obedience, is that love? Is love apprehensive? Surely, when you look up to somebody, you also look down upon somebody else, don't you? And is that love? In love is there any sense of looking up or looking down, any compulsion to obey another?

When you say you love somebody, don't you inwardly depend

on that person? While you are a child you naturally depend on your father, on your mother, on your teacher, on your guardian. You need to be cared for, to be provided with food, clothing, and shelter. You need a sense of security, the feeling that someone is looking after you.

But what generally happens? As we grow older, this feeling of dependence continues, does it not? Haven't you noticed it in older people, in your parents and teachers? Haven't you observed how they depend emotionally on their wives or husbands, on their children, or on their own parents? When they grow up, most people still cling to somebody; they continue to be dependent. Without someone to lean on, to give them a sense of comfort and security, they feel lonely, do they not? They feel lost. This dependency on another is called love; but if you observe it very closely you will see that dependency is fear, it is not love.

Most people are afraid to stand alone; they are afraid to think things out for themselves, afraid to feel deeply, to explore and discover the whole meaning of life. Therefore they say they love God, and they depend on what they call God; but it is not God, the unknown, it is a thing created by the mind.

We do the same with an ideal or a belief. I believe in something, or I hold on to an ideal, and that gives me great comfort; but remove the ideal, remove the belief and I am lost. It is the same thing with a guru. I depend because I want to receive, so there is the ache of fear. Again it is the same when you depend on your parents or teachers. It is natural and right that you should do so when you are young; but if you keep on depending when you have grown to maturity, that will make you incapable of thinking, of being free. Where there is dependence, there is fear, and where there is fear, there is authority; there is no love. When your parents say that you must obey, that you must follow certain traditions, that you must take only a certain job or do only a particular kind of work—in all this there is no love. And there is no love in your heart when you depend on society in the sense that you accept the structure of society as it is, without question.

Ambitious men and women do not know what love is—and we are dominated by ambitious people. That is why there is no happiness in the world, and why it is very important that you, as you grow up, should see and understand all this, and find out for yourself if it is possible to discover what love is. You may have a good position, a very fine house, a marvelous garden, clothes; you may become the prime minister; but without love, none of these things have any meaning.

So, you have to begin to find out now—not wait until you are old, for you will never find out then—what it is you actually feel in your relationship with your parents, with your teachers, with the guru. You cannot merely accept the word *love* or any other word, but must go behind the meaning of words to see what the reality is—the reality being that which you actually feel, not what you are supposed to feel. If you actually feel jealous, or angry, to say, "I must not be jealous, I must not be angry" is merely a wish, it has no reality. What matters is to see very honestly and very clearly exactly what it is you are feeling at the moment, without bringing in the ideal of how you *should* feel or will feel at some future date, for then you can do something about it. But to say, "I *must* love my parents, I *must* love my teachers" has no meaning, has it? Because your real feelings are quite different, and those words become a screen behind which you hide.

So, is it not the way of intelligence to look beyond the accepted meaning of words? Words like *duty, responsibility, God, love* have acquired a traditional meaning; but an intelligent person, a truly educated person, looks beyond the traditional meaning of such words. For instance, if someone told you that he did not believe in God, you would be shocked, would you not? You would say, "Goodness, how awful!" because you believe in God—at least you think you do. But belief and nonbelief have very little meaning.

What is important is for you to go behind the word *love* to see whether you actually do love your parents, and whether your parents actually do love you. Surely, if you and your parents really loved one another, the world would be entirely different. There would be no wars, no starvation, no class differences. There would be no rich and no poor. You see, without love we try to reform society economically, we try to put things right, but as long as we have no love in our hearts we cannot bring about a social structure free of conflict and misery. That is why we have to go into these things very carefully; and perhaps then we shall find out what love is.

Questioner: Why is there sorrow and misery in the world?

Krishnamurti: I wonder if that boy knows what those words mean. He has probably seen an overloaded donkey with his legs almost breaking, or another boy crying, or a mother beating her child. Perhaps he has seen older people quarrelling with each other. And there is death, the body being carried away to be burnt; there is the beggar; there is poverty, disease, old age; there is sorrow, not only outside, but also inside us. So he asks, "Why is there sorrow?" Don't you want to know too? Have you never wondered about the cause of your own sorrow? What is sorrow, and why does it exist? If I want something and cannot get it, I feel miserable; if I want more saris, more money, or if I want to be more beautiful, and cannot have what I want, I am unhappy. If I want to love a certain person and that person does not love me, again I am miserable. My father dies, and I am in sorrow. Why?

Why do we feel unhappy when we cannot have what we want? Why should we necessarily have what we want? We think it is our right, do we not? But do we ever ask ourselves why we should have what we want when millions have not got even what they *need*? And besides, why do we want it? There is our need of food, clothing, and shelter; but we are not satisfied with that. We want much more. We want success, we want to be respected, loved, looked up to, we want to be powerful, we want to be famous poets, saints, orators, we want to be prime ministers, presidents. Why? Have you ever looked into it? Why do we want all this? Not that we must be satisfied with what we are. I do not mean that. That would be ugly, silly. But why this constant craving for more and more and more? This craving indicates that we are dissatisfied, discontented, but with what? With what we are? I am *this*, I do not like it, and I want to be *that*. I think I shall look much more beautiful in a new coat or a new sari, so I want it. This means I am dissatisfied with what I am, and I think I can escape from my discontent by acquiring more clothes, more power, and so on. But the dissatisfaction is still there, is it not? I have only covered it up with clothes, with power, with cars.

So, we have to find out how to understand what we are. Merely to cover ourselves with possessions, with power and position, has no meaning, because we will still be unhappy. Seeing this, the unhappy person, the person who is in sorrow, does not run away to gurus, he does not hide in possessions, in power; on the contrary, he wants to know what lies behind his sorrow. If you go behind your own sorrow you will find that you are very small, empty, limited, and that you are struggling to achieve, to become. This very struggle to achieve, to become something, is the cause of sorrow. But if you begin to understand what you actually are, go deeper and deeper into it, then you will find that something quite different takes place.

Questioner: If a man is starving and I feel that I can be helpful to him, is this ambition or love?

Krishnamurti: It all depends on the motive with which you help him. By saying he is for helping the poor man, the politician gets to New Delhi, lives in a big house, and shows himself off. Is that love? Do you understand? Is that love?

Questioner: If I relieve his starvation by my helpfulness, isn't that love?

Krishnamurti: He is starving and you help him with food. Is that love? Why do you want to help him? Have you no motive, no incentive other than the desire to help him? Do you not get any benefit out of it? Think this out, do not say yes or no. If you are looking for some benefit out of it, politically or otherwise, some inward or outward benefit, then you do not love him. If you feed him in order to become more popular, or in the hope that your friends will help you to go to New Delhi, then that is not love, is it? But if you love him, you will feed him without any ulterior motive, without wanting anything in return. If you feed him and he is ungrateful, do you feel hurt? If so, you do not love him. If he tells you and the villagers that you are a wonderful man, and you feel very flattered, it means you are thinking about yourself; and surely that is not love. So, one has to be very alert to find out if one is deriving any kind of benefit from one's helpfulness, and what the motive is that leads one to feed the hungry.

Questioner: Suppose I want to go home and the principal says no. If I disobey him, I will have to face the consequences. If I obey the principal, it will break my heart. What am I to do?

Krishnamurti: Do you mean to say that you cannot talk it over with the principal, that you cannot take him into your confidence and show him your problem? If he is the right kind of principal you can trust him, talk over your problem with him. If he still says you must not go, it is possible that he is just being obstinate, which means there is something wrong with the principal; but he may have good reasons for saying no, and you have to find out. So it requires mutual confidence. You must have confidence in the principal, and the principal must have confidence in you. Life is not just a one-sided relationship. You are a human being; so is the principal a human being, and he also may make mistakes. So both of you must be willing to talk it over. You may want very much to go home but that may not be quite enough; your parents may have written to the principal not to let you come home. It must be a mutual inquiry, must it not?, so that you do not get hurt, so that you do not feel ill-treated or brutally pushed aside; and that can happen only when you have confidence in the teacher and he has confidence in you. In other words, there has to be real love; and such an environment is what a school should provide.

Questioner: Why should we not do *puja*?

Krishnamurti: Have you found out why the older people do *puja*? They are copying, are they not? The more immature we are, the more we want to copy. Have you noticed how people love uniforms? So, before you ask why you should not do *puja*, ask the older people why *they* do it. They do it, first of all, because it is a tradition; their grandfathers did it. Then the repetition of words gives them a certain sense of peace. Do you understand this? Words constantly repeated make the mind dull, and that gives you a sense of quietness. Sanskrit words especially have certain vibrations which make you feel very quiet. The older people also do *puja* because everybody else is doing it; and you, being young, want to copy them. Do you want to do *puja* because somebody tells you it is the right thing to do? Do you want to do it because you find a pleasant hypnotic effect in repeating certain words? Before you do anything, should you not find out why you want to do it? Even if millions of people believe in *puja*, should you not use your own mind to discover the true significance of it?

You see, the mere repetition of Sanskrit words, or of certain gestures, will not really help you to find out what truth is, what God is. To find that out, you must know how to meditate. But this is quite a different matter—quite different from doing *puja*. Millions of people do *puja*; and has it brought about a happier world? Are such people creative? To be creative is to be full of initiative, full of love, of kindness, of sympathy and consideration. If as a little boy you begin to do *puja* and go on repeating it, you will become like a machine. But if you begin to question, to doubt, to inquire, then perhaps you will find out how to meditate. And meditation, if you know how to do it properly, is one of the greatest blessings.

9

The Importance of Understanding Your Mind

I do not think we shall understand the complex problem of love till we understand the equally complex problem which we call the mind. Have you noticed, when we are very young, how inquisitive we are? We want to know, and we see many more things than the older people do. If we are at all awake, we observe things that the older people do not even notice. The mind, when we are young, is much more alert, much more curious and wanting to know. That is why we learn so easily mathematics, geography, or whatever it is. As we grow older, the mind becomes more and more crystallized, heavy, dull. Have you noticed how prejudiced most older people are? Their minds are not open, they approach everything from a fixed point of view. You are young now, but if you are not very watchful, your mind also will become like that.

Is it not then very important to understand the mind, and to see whether, instead of gradually becoming dull, you can be supple, capable of instant adjustments, of extraordinary initiative, of deep research and understanding in every department of life? Must you not know the ways of the mind to understand the way of love? Because it is the mind that destroys love. People who are merely clever, cunning, do not know what love is, because their minds, although sharp, are superficial; they live on the surface, and love is not a thing that rests on the surface.

What is the mind? I do not mean just the brain, the physical organism which reacts to stimuli through various nervous responses, and about which any physiologist can tell you. Rather we are going to find out what the mind is. The mind which says, "I think"; "it is mine"; "I am hurt"; "I am jealous"; "I love"; "I hate"; "I am an Indian"; "I am a Muslim"; "I believe in this and I do not believe in that"; "I know and you do not know"; "I respect"; "I despise"; "I want"; "I do not want"—what is this thing? Unless you begin now to understand and make yourself thoroughly familiar with the whole process of thinking which is called the mind, unless you are fully aware of it in yourself, you will gradually, as you grow older, become hard, crystallized, dull, fixed in a certain pattern of thought.

What is this thing which we call the mind? It is the way of our thinking, is it not? I am talking of *your* mind, not somebody else's mind—the way you think and feel, the way you look at the trees, at the fishermen, the way you consider the villager. Your mind, as you grow older, gradually becomes warped or fixed in a certain pattern. You want something, you crave it, you desire to be or become something, and this desire sets a pattern; that is, your mind creates a pattern and gets caught in it. Your desire crystallizes your mind.

Say, for example, you want to be a very rich man. The desire to be wealthy creates a pattern, and your thinking then gets caught in it; you can think only in those terms, and you cannot go beyond them. Therefore your mind slowly becomes crystallized, it gets hard, dull. Or, if you believe in something—in God, in Communism, in a certain political system—that very belief sets the pattern, because it is the outcome of your desire; and your desire strengthens the walls of the pattern. Gradually your mind becomes incapable of quick adjustment, of deep penetration, of real clarity, because you are caught in the labyrinth of your own desires.

So, until we begin to investigate this process which we call the mind, until we are familiar with and understand our own ways of thinking, we cannot possibly find out what love is. There can be no love as long as our minds desire certain things of love, or demand that it act in a certain way. When we imagine what love should be and give to it certain motives, we gradually create a pattern of action with regard to love; but that is not love, it is merely our idea of what love should be.

Say, for example, I possess my wife or husband, as you possess a sari or a coat. If somebody took away your coat, you would be anxious, irritated, angry. Why? Because you regard that coat as your property; you possess it, and through its possession you feel enriched, don't you? Through possessing many clothes you feel enriched, not only physically but inwardly; and when somebody takes away your coat, you feel irritated because inwardly you are being deprived of that feeling of richness, that sense of possession.

Now, the feeling of possession creates a barrier with regard to love, does it not? If I own you, possess you, is that love? I possess you as I possess a car, a coat, a sari, because in possessing, I feel very gratified, and I depend on that feeling; it is very important to me inwardly. This sense of owning, possessing someone, this emotional dependence on another, is what we call love; but if you examine it, you will find that, behind the word *love*, the mind is taking satisfaction in possession. After all, when you possess many beautiful saris, or a fine car, or a big house, the feeling that it is yours inwardly gives you great satisfaction.

So, in desiring, wanting, the mind creates a pattern, and in that pattern it gets caught; and then it grows weary, dull, stupid, thoughtless. The mind is the center of this feeling of possession, the feeling of the 'me' and the 'mine': "I own something," "I am a big man," "I am a little man," "I am insulted," "I am flattered," "I am clever," "I am very beautiful," "I want to be somebody," "I am the son or the daughter of somebody." This feeling of the 'me' and the 'mine' is the very core of the mind, it is the mind itself. The more the mind has this feeling of being somebody, of being great, or very clever, or very stupid, and so on, the more it builds walls around itself and becomes enclosed, dull. Then it suffers, for in that enclosure inevitably there is pain. Because it is suffering, the mind says, "What am I to do?" But instead of removing the enclosing walls by awareness, by careful thought, by going into and understanding the whole process by which they are created, it struggles to find something else outside with which to enclose itself again. So the mind gradually becomes a barrier to love; and without understanding what the mind is, which is to understand the ways of our own thinking, the inner source from which there is action, we cannot possibly find out what love is.

Is not the mind also an instrument of comparison? You know what it means to compare. You say, "This is better than that"; you compare yourself with somebody who is more beautiful, or less clever. There is comparison when you say, "I remember a river which I saw a year ago, and it is still more beautiful than this one." You compare yourself with a saint or a hero, with the ultimate ideal. This comparative judgment makes the mind dull; it does not quicken the mind, it does not make the mind comprehensive, inclusive. When you are constantly comparing, what happens? When you see the sunset and immediately compare it with a previous sunset, or when you say, "That mountain is beautiful, but I saw a still more beautiful mountain two years ago," you are really not looking at the beauty which is there before you. So comparison prevents you from looking fully. If, in looking at you, I say, "I know a much nicer person," I am not really looking at you, am I? My mind is occupied with something else. To really look at a sunset, there must be no comparison; to really look at you, I must not compare you with someone else. It is only when I look at you fully, not with comparative judgment, that I can understand you. When I compare you with another, I do not understand you, I merely judge you, I say you are this or that. So stupidity arises when there is comparison, because in comparing you with somebody else there is a lack of human dignity. But when I look at you without comparing, then my only concern is to understand you, and in that very concern, which is not comparative, there is intelligence, there is human dignity.

As long as the mind is comparing, there is no love; and the mind is always comparing, weighing, judging, is it not? It is always looking to find out where the weakness is, so there is no love. When the mother and father love their children, they do not compare one child with another. But you compare yourself with someone better, nobler, richer; you are all the time concerned with yourself in relation to somebody else, so you create in yourself a lack of love. In this way the mind becomes more and more comparative, more and more possessive, more and more dependent, thereby establishing a pattern in which it gets caught. Because it cannot look at anything anew, afresh, it destroys the very perfume of life, which is love.

Questioner: What should we ask God to give us?

Krishnamurti: You are very interested in God, are you not? Why? Because your mind is asking for something, wanting something. So it is constantly agitated. If I am asking or expecting something from you, my mind is agitated, is it not?

This boy wants to know what he should ask of God. He does not know what God is, or what it is he really wants. But there is a general feeling of apprehension, the feeling, "I must ask, I must pray, I must be protected." The mind is always seeking in every corner to get something; it is always wanting, grasping, watching, pushing, comparing, judging, and so it is never still. Observe your own mind and you will see what it is doing, how it tries to control itself, to dominate, to suppress, to find some form of satisfaction, how it is constantly asking, begging, struggling, comparing. We call such a mind very alert, but is it alert? Surely, an alert mind is a still mind, not one that, like a butterfly, is chasing all over the place. And it is only a still mind that can understand what God is. A still mind never asks anything of God. It is only the impoverished mind that begs, that asks. What it asks, it can never have, because what it really wants is security, comfort, certainty. If you ask anything of God, you will never find God.

Questioner: What is real greatness and how can I be great?

Krishnamurti: You see, the unfortunate thing is that we want to be great. We all want to be great. We want to be a Gandhi or a prime minister, we want to be great inventors, great writers. Why? In education, in religion, in all the departments of our life, we have examples. The great poet, the great orator, the great statesman, the great saint, the great hero—such people are held up as examples, and we want to be like them.

Now, when you want to be like another, you have created a pattern of action, have you not? You have set a limitation on your thought, bound it within certain limits. So your thought has already become crystallized, narrow, limited, stifled. Why do you want to be great? Why do you not look at what you are and understand that? You see, the moment you want to be like another, there is misery, conflict, there is envy, sorrow. If you want to be like the Buddha, what happens? You struggle everlastingly to achieve that ideal. If you are stupid and crave to be clever, you constantly try to leave what you are and go beyond it. If you are ugly and want to be beautiful, you long to be beautiful till you die, or you deceive yourself into thinking you are beautiful. So, as long as you are trying to be something other than what you actually are, your mind merely wears itself out. But if you say, "This is what I am, it is a fact, and I am going to investigate, understand it," then you can go beyond; for you will find that the understanding of what you are brings great peace and contentment, great insight, great love.

Questioner: Is not love based on attraction?

Krishnamurti: Suppose you are attracted to a beautiful woman or a handsome man. What is wrong with that? We are trying to find out. You see, when you are attracted to a woman, to a man, or to a child, what generally happens? You not only want to be with that person, but you want to possess, to call that person your own. Your body must be near that person's body. So what have you done? The fact is that when you are attracted, you want to possess, you do not want that person to look at anybody else;

and when you consider another human being as yours, is there love? Obviously not. The moment your mind creates a hedge as the 'mine' around that person, there is no love.

The fact is that our minds are doing this all the time. That is why we are discussing these things—to see how the mind is working; and perhaps, being aware of its own movements, the mind will be quiet of its own accord.

Questioner: What is prayer? Has it any importance in daily life?

Krishnamurti: Why do you pray? And what is prayer? Most prayer is merely a petitioning, an asking. You indulge in this kind of prayer when you suffer. When you feel all alone, when you are depressed and in sorrow, you ask God for help; so what you call prayer is a petition. The form of prayer may vary, but the intent behind it is generally the same. Prayer, with most people, is a petition, a begging, an asking. Are you doing that? Why do you pray? I am not saying that you should or should not pray. But why do you pray? Is it for more knowledge, for more peace? Do you pray that the world may be free from sorrow? Is there any other kind of prayer? There is prayer which is really not a prayer, but the sending out of goodwill, the sending out of love, the sending out of ideas. What is it you are doing?

When you pray, generally you are asking God, or some saint, to fill your empty bowl, are you not? You are not satisfied with what happens, with what is given, but you want your bowl filled according to your wishes. So your prayer is merely a petition, it is a demand that you should be satisfied, therefore it is not prayer at all. You say to God, "I am suffering, please gratify me; please give me back my brother, my son. Please make me rich." You are per-petuating your own demands, and that is obviously not prayer.

The real thing is to understand yourself, to see why you are perpetually asking for something, why there is in you this demand, this urge to beg. The more you know yourself through awareness of what you are thinking, what you are feeling, the more you will discover the truth of *what is*; and it is this truth that will help you to be free.

10

On How to Listen

I think it is very important to know how to listen. If you know how to listen, you will get to the root of the matter immediately. If you listen to pure sound, you have immediate contact with the beauty of it. Similarly, if you knew how to listen to what is being said, there would be an immediate understanding. Listening is the complete focusing of attention. You think that attention is a tiresome thing, that to learn to concentrate is a drawn-out process. But if you really know how to listen, then attention is not difficult, and you will find that you get to the heart of the matter immediately with an extraordinary alertness.

Most of us do not really listen. We are distracted by external noises, or we have some prejudice, some bias which gives a twist to the mind, and this prevents us from really listening to what is being said. This is especially so with older people, because they have a long series of achievements and failures behind them; they are somebodies or nobodies in the world, and it is very difficult to penetrate the layers of their formulations, their preconceptions. Their imagination, their conditioning, their sense of achievement will not allow that which is being said to penetrate. But if we know how to listen to what is being said, if we can listen to it without any barrier, without any interpretation, just listen as we would to the song of a bird in the morning, then listening is an extraordinary thing, especially when something true is being said. We may not like it, we may instinctively resist it; but if we can really listen, we will see the truth of it. So real listening unburdens the mind, it clears away the dross of many years of failure, of success, of longing.

You know what propaganda is, don't you? It is to propagate, to sow or constantly repeat an idea. That is how the propagandist, the politician, the religious leader imprints on your mind what he wants you to believe. There is a listening involved in this process also. Such people constantly repeat what you should do, what books you should read, whom you should follow, which ideas are right and which are wrong; and this constant repetition leaves a mark on your mind. Even if you do not consciously listen, it is making an imprint, and that is the purpose of propaganda. But you see, propaganda is merely vested interest, it does not bring that truth which you immediately understand when you are really listening, when you are paying attention without effort.

You are now listening to me; you are not making an effort to pay attention, you are just listening; and if there is truth in what you hear, you will find a remarkable change taking place in you—a change that is not premeditated or wished for, a transformation, a complete revolution in which the truth alone is master and not the creations of your mind. And if I may suggest it, you should listen in that way to everything—not only to what I am saying, but also to what other people are saying, to the birds, to the whistle of a locomotive, to the noise of the bus going by. You will find that the more you listen to everything, the greater is the silence, and that silence is then not broken by noise. It is only when you are resisting something, when you are putting up a barrier between yourself and that to which you do not want to listen—it is only then that there is a struggle.

Now, is it not very important to be refined, both outwardly and inwardly? Do you know what refinement is? It is to be sensitive to everything about you, and also to the thoughts, the beliefs, the feelings that you have within yourself. Refinement is reflected in your clothes, in your manners, in your gestures, in the way you walk, the way you talk, the way you look at people. And refinement is essential, is it not? For without refinement, there is deterioration.

Do you know what it means to deteriorate? It is the opposite of creating, or building, of having the initiative to move forward, to develop. Deterioration implies slow decay, a withering away—and that is what is happening in the world. In colleges and universities, among nations, among people, in the individual, there is a slow decay; the deteriorating process is going on all the time, and this is because there is no inward refinement. You may have a certain amount of outward refinement, you may wear fine clothes, live in a nice house, eat good food, observe scrupulous cleanliness; but without inner refinement, the outward perfection of form has very little meaning. It is merely another form of deterioration. To have beautiful possessions but to be inwardly gross, that is, to be concerned with one's own vanity and grandeur, with one's ambitions and achievements, is the way of deterioration.

There is beauty of form in poetry, or in a person, or in a lovely tree, but it has meaning only through the inward refinement of love. If there is love, there will be outward as well as inward refinement. Refinement is expressed outwardly in consideration for others, in the way you treat your parents, your neighbors, your servant, your gardener. The gardener may have created for you a beautiful garden, but without that refinement which is love, the garden is merely an expression of your own vanity.

So, it is essential to have both outward and inward refinement. The way you eat matters a great deal; if you make a noise while you are eating, it matters very much. The way you behave, your manners when you are with your friends, the way you talk about others, all these things matter because they point to what you are inwardly, they indicate whether or not there is inward refinement. A lack of inward refinement expresses itself in the outward degeneration of form; so outward refinement has very little meaning if there is no love. And we have seen that love is not a thing we can possess. It comes into being only when the mind understands the complex problems which it has itself created.

Questioner: Why do we feel a sense of pride when we succeed?

Krishnamurti: With success is there a sense of pride? What is success? Have you ever considered what it is to be successful as a writer, as a poet, as a painter, as a business man or politician? To feel that you have inwardly achieved a certain control over yourself which others do not have, or that you have succeeded where others have failed; to feel that you are better than somebody else, that you have become a successful man, that you are respected, looked up to by others as an example—what does all this indicate? Naturally, when you have this feeling, there is pride: *I* have done something, *I* am important. The feeling of 'I' is in its very nature a sense of pride. So pride grows with success; one is proud of being very important compared with other people. This comparison of yourself with another exists also in your pursuit of the example, the ideal, and it gives you hope, it gives you strength, purpose, drive, which only strengthens the 'I', the pleasurable feeling that you are much more important than anybody else; and that feeling, that sense of pleasure, is the beginning of pride.

Pride brings a great deal of vanity, an egotistic inflation. You can observe this in the older people and in yourself. When you pass an examination and feel that you are a little cleverer than another, a sense of pleasure comes in. It is the same when you outdo somebody in an argument, or when you feel that you are physically much stronger or more beautiful—immediately there is a sense of your own importance. This feeling of the importance of the 'me' inevitably brings conflict, struggle, pain, because you have to maintain your importance all the time.

Questioner: How can we be free of pride?

Krishnamurti: If you had really listened to the answer to the previous question, you would have understood how to be free of pride, and you would be free of pride; but you were concerned with how to put the next question, were you not? So you were not listening. If you really listen to what is being said, you will find out for yourself the truth of it.

Suppose I am proud because I have achieved something. I have become the principal; I have been to England or to America; I have done great things, my photograph has appeared in the newspapers, and so on and so on. Feeling very proud, I say to myself, "How am I to be free of pride?"

Now, why do I want to be free of pride? That is the important question, not *how* to be free. What is the motive, what is the reason, what is the incentive? Do I want to be free of pride because I find it harmful to me, painful, spiritually not good? If that is the motive, then to try to free myself from pride is another form of pride, is it not? I am still concerned with achievement. Finding that pride is very painful, spiritually ugly, I say that I must be free of it. The 'I must be free' contains the same motive as the 'I must be successful'. The 'I' is still important, it is the centre of my struggle to be free.

So, what matters is not how to be free of pride, but to understand the 'I'; and the 'I' is very subtle. It wants one thing this year and another thing next year; and when that turns out to be painful, it then wants something else. So, as long as the center of the 'I' exists, whether one is proud or so-called humble is of very little significance. They are only different coats to put on. When a particular coat appeals to me, I put it on; and next year, according to my fancies, my desires, I put on another coat.

What you have to understand is how this 'I' comes into being. The 'I' comes into being through the sense of achievement in various forms. This does not mean that you must not act; but the feeling that *you* are acting, that *you* are achieving, that *you* must be without pride, has to be understood. You have to understand the structure of the 'I'. You have to be aware of your own thinking; you have to observe how you treat your servant, your mother and father, your teacher and the servant; you have to be conscious of how you regard those who are above you and those who are below you, those whom you respect and those whom you despise. All this reveals the ways of the 'I'. Through understanding the ways of the 'I' there is freedom from the 'I'. *That* is what matters, not just how to be free of pride.

Questioner: How can a thing of beauty be a joy forever?

Krishnamurti: Is that your original thought, or are you quoting somebody? Do you want to find out if beauty is perishable, and whether there can be everlasting joy?

Questioner: Beauty comes in certain forms.

Krishnamurti: The tree, the leaf, the river, the woman, the man, those villagers carrying a burden on their heads and walking beautifully. Is beauty perishable?

Questioner: The villagers walk by, but they leave an impression of beauty.

Krishnamurti: They walk by, and the memory of it remains. You see a tree, a leaf, and the memory of that beauty remains.

Now, is the memory of beauty a living thing? When you see something beautiful, there is immediate joy; you see a sunset and there is an immediate response of joy. That joy, a few moments later, has become a memory. Is the memory of that joy a living thing? Is your memory of the sunset a living thing? It is a dead imprint, is it not? And through that dead imprint of the sunset, you want to recapture the joy. But memory has no joy; it is only the image of something which has gone and which once created joy. There is joy as the immediate response to beauty, but memory comes in and destroys it. If there is constant perception of beauty without the accumulations of memory—only then is there a possibility of joy everlasting.

But it is not easy to be free from the accumulations of memory, because the moment you see something very pleasurable, you make it into a memory which you hold on to. When you see a beautiful object, a beautiful child, a beautiful tree, there is immediate joy; but then you want more of it. Wanting more of it is the accumulation of memory. In wanting more you have already started the process of disintegration, and in that there is no joy. Memory can never produce everlasting joy. There is everlasting joy only when there is a constant and spontaneous response to beauty, to ugliness, to everything, without the activating impulse of memory—which implies great inward and outward sensitivity, having real love.

Questioner: Why are the poor happy and the rich unhappy?

Krishnamurti: Are the poor particularly happy? They may sing, they may dance; but are they happy? They have insufficient food, they have little or no clothing, they cannot be clean, they have to work from morning till night year after year. They may have occasional moments of happiness; but they are not really happy, are they?

And are the rich unhappy? They have an abundance of everything, they have high positions, they travel. They are unhappy when they are frustrated in some way, when they are hindered and cannot get what they want.

What do you mean by happiness? Some will say that happiness consists in getting what you want. If you want a car and you get it, you are happy, at least for the time being. It is the same whether you want a sari, or a trip to Europe: if you can get what you want, you are happy. If you want to be the best-known professor, or the greatest politician, you are happy if you can get there, and unhappy if you cannot.

So, what you call happiness is the outcome of getting what you want, of achieving success, or becoming noble. You want something, and as long as you can get it you feel perfectly happy, you are not frustrated; but if you cannot get what you want, then unhappiness begins.

All of us are concerned with this problem, not only the rich and the poor. The rich and the poor alike want to get something for themselves, and if they are prevented, they are unhappy. I am not saying that the poor should not have what they want or need. That is not the question we are considering. We are trying to find out what happiness is, and whether happiness is something of which you are conscious.

When you are conscious that you are happy, is that happiness? It is not happiness, is it? It is like humility: the moment you are conscious that you are humble, you are not humble. So you cannot go after happiness; it is not a thing to be pursued. It comes; but if you seek it, it will elude you.

Questioner: Though there is progress in different directions, why is there no brotherhood?

Krishnamurti: What do you mean by *progress?*

Questioner: Scientific progress.

Krishnamurti: From the bullock cart to the jet plane—that is progress, is it not? Centuries ago there was only the bullock cart; but gradually, through time, we have developed the jet plane. The means of transport in ancient times was very slow, and now it is very rapid; you can be in London within a few hours. Through sanitation, through proper nutrition and medical care, there has been a great improvement also in matters of physical health. All this is scientific progress; and yet we are not developing or progressing equally in brotherhood.

Now, is brotherhood a matter of progress? We know what we mean by *progress.* It is evolution, achieving something through time. The scientists say that we have evolved from the monkey; they say that, through millions of years, we have progressed from the lowest forms of life to the highest, which is man. But is brotherhood a matter of progress? Is it something which can be evolved through time? There is the unity of the family and the unity of a particular society or nation; from the nation the next step is internationalism, and then comes the idea of one world. The one-world concept is what we call brotherhood. But is brotherly feeling a matter of evolution? Is the feeling of brotherhood to be slowly cultivated through the stages of family, community, nationalism, internationalism, and world unity? Brotherliness is love, is it not? And is love to be cultivated step by step? Is love a matter of time? Do you understand what I am talking about?

If I say there will be brotherhood in ten or thirty or a hundred years, what does that indicate? It indicates, surely, that I do not love, I do not feel brotherly. When I say, "I will be brotherly, I will love," the actual fact is that I do *not* love, I am *not* brotherly. As long as I think in terms of 'I will be', I am not. Whereas, if I remove from my mind this concept of being brotherly in the future, then I can see what I actually am; I can see that I am *not* brotherly, and begin to find out why.

Which is important, to see what I am, or to speculate about what I *will* be? Surely, the important thing is to see what I am, because then I can deal with it. What I *will* be is in the future, and the future is unpredictable. The actual fact is that I have no brotherly feeling, I do not really love; and with that fact I can begin, I can immediately do something about it. But to say that one will be something in the future is mere idealism, and the idealist is an individual who is escaping from *what is*; he is running away from the fact, which can be altered only in the present.

II

Knowledge Is Not Everything

You will remember that we have been talking about fear. Now, is not fear responsible for the accumulation of knowledge? This is a difficult subject, so let us see if we can go into it, let us consider it very carefully.

Human beings accumulate and worship knowledge, not only scientific but so-called spiritual knowledge. They think that knowledge is so important in life—knowledge of what has happened, and of what is going to happen. This whole process of accumulating information, worshipping knowledge—does it not arise from the background of fear? We are afraid that without knowledge we would be lost, we would not know how to conduct ourselves. So, through reading what the sages have said, through other people's beliefs and experiences, and also through our own experiences, we gradually build up a background of knowledge which becomes tradition; and behind this tradition we take refuge. We think this knowledge or tradition is essential, and that without it we would be lost, we would not know what to do.

Now, when we talk about knowledge, what do we mean by that word? What is it that we know? What do you really know, when you come to consider the knowledge you have accumulated? At a certain level, in science, engineering, and so on, knowledge is important; but beyond that, what is it that we know?

Have you ever considered this process of accumulating knowledge? Why is it that you study, why do you pass examinations? Knowledge is necessary at a certain level, is it not? Without a knowledge of mathematics and other subjects, one could not be an engineer or a scientist. Social relationship is built upon such knowledge, and we would not be able to earn a livelihood without it. But beyond that kind of knowledge, what do we know? Beyond that, what is the nature of knowledge?

What do we mean when we say that knowledge is necessary to find God, or that knowledge is necessary to understand oneself, or that knowledge is essential to find a way through all the turmoils of life? Here we mean knowledge as experience; and what is this experience? What is it that we know through experience? Is not this knowledge used by the ego, by the 'me', to strengthen itself?

Say, for instance, that I have achieved a certain social standing. This experience, with its feelings of success, of prestige, of power, gives me a certain sense of assurance, of comfort. So the knowledge of my success, the knowledge that I am somebody, that I have position, power, strengthens the 'me', the ego, does it not?

Have you not noticed how knowledge-puffed the pundits are, or how knowledge gives to your father, your mother, your teacher the attitude, "I have experienced more than you have; I know and you do not"? So knowledge, which is merely information, gradually becomes the sustenance of vanity, the nourishment of the ego, the 'me'. For the ego cannot exist without this or some other form of parasitical dependence.

The scientist uses his knowledge to feed his vanity, to feel that he is somebody, just as the pundit does. Teachers, parents, gurus—they all want to be somebody in this world, so they use knowledge as a means to that end, to fulfill that desire; and when you go behind their words, what is it that they really know? They know only what the books contain, or what they have experienced; and their experiences depend on the background of their conditioning. Like them, most of us are filled with words, with information which we call knowledge, and without it we are lost; so there is always fear lurking behind this screen of words, of information.

Where there is fear, there is no love; and knowledge without love destroys us. That is what is happening in the world at the present time. For example, we now have sufficient knowledge to feed human beings throughout the world; we know how to feed, clothe, and shelter mankind, but we are not doing it because we are divided into nationalistic groups, each with its own egotistic pursuits. If we really had the desire to stop war, we could do so; but we have not that desire, and for the same reason. So knowledge without love becomes a means of destruction. Until we understand this, merely to pass examinations and achieve positions of prestige and power inevitably leads to deterioration, to corruption, to the slow withering away of human dignity.

It is obviously essential to have knowledge at certain levels, but it is even more important to see how knowledge is used egotistically, for selfish purposes. Observe yourself and you will see how experience is employed by the mind as a means of self-expansion, as a means of power and prestige. Watch the grown-ups and you will see how they hanker after position and cling to their success. They want to build a nest of safety for themselves, they want power, prestige, authority—and most of us, in various ways, are after the same thing. We don't want to be ourselves,

whatever we are; we want to be somebodies. There is a difference, surely, between being and wanting to be. The desire to be
or to become is continued and strengthened through knowledge, which is used for self-aggrandizement.

It is important for all of us, as we are maturing, to go into
these problems and understand them, so that we do not respect
a person merely because he has a title or a high position, or is
supposed to have a great deal of knowledge. Actually, we know
very little. We may have read many books, but very few have
direct experience of anything. It is the direct experiencing of
Reality, of God, that is of vital importance; and for that, there
must be love.

12

The Quality of Real Affection

Is it not very important, while we are young, to be loved, and also to know what it means to love? But it seems to me that most of us do not love, nor are we loved. And I think it is essential, while we are young, to go into this problem very seriously and understand it; for then perhaps we can be sensitive enough to feel love, to know its quality, its perfume, so that when we grow older it will not be entirely destroyed. So let us consider this question.

What does it mean to love? Is it an ideal, something far away, unattainable? Or can love be felt by each one of us at odd moments of the day? To have the quality of sympathy, of understanding, to help someone naturally, without any motive, to be spontaneously kind, to care for a plant or a dog, to be sympathetic to the villager, generous to your friend, to a neighbor—is this not what we mean by love? Is not love a state in which there is no sense of resentment, but everlasting forgiveness? And is it not possible while we are young to feel it?

While we are young many of us do experience this feeling—a sudden outgoing sympathy for the villager, for a dog, for those who are little or helpless. And should it not be constantly tended? Should you not always give some part of the day to aiding another, to caring for a tree or a garden, to helping in the house or in the hostel, so that, as you grow to maturity, you will know what it means to be considerate naturally, without enforcement, without motive? Should you not have this quality of real affection?

Real affection cannot be brought into being artificially, you have to *feel* it; and your guardian, your parents, your teachers must also feel it. Most people have no real affection; they are too concerned with their achievements, their longings, their knowledge, their success. They give to what they have done and want to do such colossal importance that it ultimately destroys them.

That is why it is very important, while you are young, to help look after the rooms, or to care for a number of trees which you yourself have planted, or to go to the assistance of a sick friend, so that there is a subtle feeling of sympathy, of concern, of generosity—real generosity which is not just of the mind, and which makes you want to share with somebody whatever you may have, however little. If you do not have this feeling of love, of generosity, of kindness, of gentleness, while you are young, it will be very difficult to have it when you are older; but if you begin to have it now, then perhaps you can awaken it in others.

To have sympathy and affection implies freedom from fear, does it not? But you see, it is very difficult to grow up in this world without fear, without having some personal motive in action. The older people have never thought about this problem of fear, or they have thought about it only abstractly, without acting upon it in daily existence. You are still very young, you are watching, inquiring, learning, but if you do not see and understand what causes fear, you will become as they are. Like some hidden weed, fear will grow and spread and twist your mind. You should therefore be aware of everything that is happening around you and within yourself—how the teachers talk, how our parents behave, and how you respond—so that this question of fear is seen and understood.

Most grown-up people think that some kind of discipline is necessary. Do you know what discipline is? It is a process of making you do something which you do not want to do. Where there is discipline, there is fear; so discipline is not the way of love. That is why discipline at all costs should be avoided—discipline being coercion, resistance, compulsion, making you do something which you really do not understand, or persuading you to do it by offering you a reward. If you don't understand something, don't do it, and don't be compelled to do it. Ask for an explanation; don't just be obstinate, but try to find out the truth of the matter so that no fear is involved and your mind becomes very pliable, very supple.

When you do not understand and are merely compelled by the authority of grown-up people, you are suppressing your own mind, and then fear comes into being; and that fear pursues you like a shadow throughout life. That is why it is so important not to be disciplined according to any particular type of thought or pattern of action. But most older people can think only in those terms. They want to make you do something for your so-called good. This very process of making you do something for your own "good" destroys your sensitivity, your capacity to understand, and therefore your love. To refuse to be coerced or compelled is very difficult, because the world about us is so strong; but if we merely give in and do things without understanding, we fall into a habit of thoughtlessness, and then it becomes still more difficult for us to break away.

So, in your school, should you have authority, discipline? Or should you be encouraged by your teachers to discuss these questions, go into them, understand them so that, when you are grown up and go out into the world, you will be a mature human being who is capable of meeting intelligently the world's problems? You cannot have that deep intelligence if there is any kind of fear. Fear only makes you dull, it curbs your initiative, it destroys that flame which we call sympathy, generosity, affection, love. So do not allow yourself to be disciplined into a pattern of action, but find out—which means that you must have the time to question, to inquire; and the teachers must also have the time; if there is no time, then time must be made. Fear is a source of corruption, it is the beginning of degeneration, and to be free of fear is more important than any examination or any scholastic degree.

Questioner: What is love in itself?

Krishnamurti: What is intrinsic love? Is that what you mean? What is love without motive, without incentive? Listen carefully and you will find out. We are examining the question, we are not looking for the answer. In studying mathematics, or in putting a question, most of you are more concerned with finding the answer than with understanding the problem. If you study the problem, look into it, examine it, understand it, you will find that the answer is in the problem. So let us understand what the problem is, and not look for an answer, either in the Bhagavad Gita, in the Koran, in the Bible, or from some professor or lecturer. If we can really understand the problem, the answer will come out of it; because the answer is in the problem, it is not separate from the problem.

The problem is: what is love without motive? Can there be love without any incentive, without wanting something for oneself out of love? Can there be love in which there is no sense of being wounded when love is not returned? If I offer you my friendship and you turn away, am I not hurt? Is that feeling of being hurt the outcome of friendship, of generosity, of sympathy? Surely, as long as I feel hurt, as long as there is fear, as long as I help you hoping that you may help me—which is called service—there is no love.

If you understand this, the answer is there.

Questioner: What is religion?

Krishnamurti: Do you want an answer from me, or do you want to find out for yourself? Are you looking for an answer from somebody, however great or however stupid? Or are you really trying to find out the truth of what religion is?

To find out what true religion is, you have to push aside everything that stands in the way. If you have many colored or dirty windows and you want to see the clear sunlight, you must clean or open the windows, or go outside. Similarly, to find out what true religion is, you must first see what it is *not*, and put that aside. Then you can find out, because then there is direct perception. So let us see what is not religion.

Doing *puja*, performing a ritual—is that religion? You repeat over and over again a certain ritual, a certain *mantram* in front of an altar or an idol. It may give you a sense of pleasure, a sense of satisfaction, but is that religion? Putting on the sacred thread, calling yourself a Hindu, a Buddhist, or a Christian, accepting certain traditions, dogmas, beliefs—has all this got anything to do with religion? Obviously not. So religion must be something which can be found only when the mind has understood and put all this aside.

Religion, in the true sense of the word, does not bring about separation, does it? But what happens when you are a Muslim and I am a Christian, or when I believe in something and you do not believe in it? Our beliefs separate us; therefore our beliefs have nothing to do with religion. Whether we believe in God or do not believe in God has very little significance; because what we believe or disbelieve is determined by our conditioning, is it not? The society around us, the culture in which we are brought up, imprints upon the mind certain beliefs, fears, and superstitions which we call religion; but they have nothing to do with religion. The fact that you believe in one way and I in another largely depends on where we happen to have been born, whether in England, in India, in Russia or America. So belief is not religion, it is only the result of our conditioning.

Then there is the pursuit of personal salvation. I want to be safe; I want to reach nirvana, or heaven; I must find a place next to Jesus, next to Buddha, or on the right hand of a particular God. Your belief does not give me deep satisfaction, comfort, so I have my own belief which does. And is that religion? Surely, one's mind must be free of all these things to find out what true religion is.

And is religion merely a matter of doing good, of serving or helping others? Or is it something more? Which does not mean that we must not be generous or kind. But is that all? Is not religion something much greater, much purer, vaster, more expansive than anything conceived by the mind?

So, to discover what is true religion, you must inquire deeply into all these things and be free of fear. It is like going out of a dark house into the sunshine. Then you will not ask what is true religion; you will know. There will be the direct experiencing of that which is true.

Questioner: If somebody is unhappy and wants to be happy, is that ambition?

Krishnamurti: When you are suffering, you want to be free of suffering. That is not ambition, is it? That is the natural instinct of every person. It is the natural instinct of us all not to have fear, not to have physical or emotional pain. But our life is such that we are constantly experiencing pain. I eat something which does not agree with me, and I have a tummy-ache. Somebody says something to me, and I feel hurt. I am prevented from doing something which I long to do, and I feel frustrated, miserable. I am unhappy because my father or my son is dead, and so on. Life is constantly acting upon me, whether I like it or not, and I am always getting hurt, frustrated, having painful reactions. So what I have to do is to understand this whole process. But, you see, most of us run away from it.

When you suffer inwardly, psychologically, what do you do? You look to somebody for consolation; you read a book, or turn on the radio, or go and do *puja*. These are all indications of your running away from suffering. If you run away from something, obviously you do not understand it. But if you look at your suffering, observe it from moment to moment, you begin to understand the problem involved in it, and this is not ambition. Ambition arises when you run away from your suffering, or when you cling to it, or when you fight it, or when around it you gradually build theories and hopes. The moment you run away from suffering, the thing to which you run becomes very important because you identify yourself with it. You identify yourself with your country, with your position, with your God, and this is a form of ambition.

13

Understanding Is Not Memorizing

What I am saying in all these talks is not something to be merely remembered. It is not intended that you should try to store in your mind what you hear, to be recollected and either thought about or acted upon later. If you merely store in your mind what I am telling you, it will be nothing but memory; it won't be a living thing, something which you really understand. It is understanding that matters, not recollection. I hope you see the difference between the two. Understanding is immediate, direct, it is something which you experience intensely. But if you merely remember what you have heard, it will only serve as a pattern, a guide to be followed, a slogan to be repeated, an idea to be imitated, an ideal on which to base your life. Understanding is not a matter of remembrance. It is a continuous intensity, a constant discovery.

So, if you merely remember what I am talking about, you will compare and try to modify your action or adjust it to what you remember. But if you really understand, that very understanding brings about action, and then you do not have to act according to your remembrance. That is why it is very important not just to remember, but to listen and understand immediately.

When you remember certain words, certain phrases, or recall certain feelings that are awakened here, and compare your action with what you remember, there is always a gap between your action and what is remembered. But if you really understand, there is no copying. Anyone with a certain capacity can remember words and pass examinations; but if you begin to understand all that is involved in what you see, in what you hear, in what you feel, that very understanding brings about an action which you do not have to guide, shape, or control.

If you merely remember, you will always be comparing; and comparison breeds envy, on which our whole acquisitive society is based. Comparison will never bring about understanding. In understanding there is love, whereas comparison is mere intellectualization; it is a mental process of imitating, following, and in which there is always the danger of the leader and the led. Do you see this?

In this world, the structure of society is based on the leader and the led, the example and the one who follows the example, the hero and the worshipper of the hero. If you go behind this process of leading and being led, you will find that when you follow another, there is no initiative. There is no freedom either for you or for the leader; because you create the leader, and the leader then controls you. As long as you are following an example of self-sacrifice, of greatness, of wisdom, of love, as long as you have an ideal to be remembered and copied there will inevitably be a gap, a division between the ideal and your action. A man who really sees the truth of this has no ideal, no example; he is not following anybody. For him there is no guru, no mahatma, no heroic leader. He is constantly understanding what lies within himself and what he hears from others, whether it be from his father or mother, from a teacher, or from a person like myself who occasionally comes into his life.

If you are now listening and understanding, then you are not following or imitating; therefore there is no fear, and so there is love.

It is very important to see all this very clearly for yourself, so that you are not bewitched by heroes or mesmerized by examples, ideals. Examples, heroes, ideals have to be remembered and are easily forgotten; therefore you have to have a constant reminder in the form of a picture, an idol, a slogan. In following an ideal, an example, you are merely remembering; and in remembrance there is no understanding. You are comparing what you are with what you want to be, and that very comparison breeds authority; it breeds envy and fear, in which there is no love.

Please listen to all this very carefully and understand it, so that you have no leaders to follow, no examples, no ideals to imitate or copy; for then you are a free individual with human dignity. You cannot be free if you are everlastingly comparing yourself with the ideal, with what you *should* be. To understand what you actually are—however ugly or beautiful, or however frightened you may be—is not a matter of remembrance, the mere recollection of an ideal. You have to watch, to be aware of yourself from moment to moment in daily relationship. To be conscious of what you actually *are* is the process of understanding.

If you really understand what I am talking about, listen to it completely, you will be free of all the utterly false things that past generations have created. You will not be burdened with imitation, the mere recollection of an ideal, which only cripples the mind and heart, breeding fear and envy. Unconsciously you may be listening to all this very deeply. I hope you are; for then you will see what an extraordinary transformation comes with deep listening and freedom from imitation.

Questioner: Is beauty subjective or objective?

Krishnamurti: You see something beautiful, the river from the verandah; or you see a child in tatters, crying. If you are not sensitive, if you are not aware of everything around you, then you just pass by and that incident is of very little value. A woman comes along carrying a burden on her head. Her clothes are dirty; she is hungry and tired. Are you aware of the beauty of her walk, or sensitive to her physical state? Do you see the color of her sari, however soiled it may be? There are these objective influences all about you; and if you have no sensitivity, you will never appreciate them, will you?

To be sensitive is to be aware not only of the things which are called beautiful, but also of that which is called ugly. The river, the green fields, the trees in the distance, the clouds of an evening— these things we call beautiful. The dirty, half-starved villagers, the people who live in squalor, or who have very little capacity for thought, very little feeling—all this we call ugly. Now, if you observe you will see that what most of us do is to cling to the beautiful and shut out the ugly. But is it not important to be sensitive to what is called ugliness as well as to beauty? It is the lack of this sensitivity that causes us to divide life into the ugly and the beautiful. But if we are open, receptive, sensitive to the ugly as well as to the beautiful, then we shall see that they are both full of meaning, and this perception gives enrichment to life.

So, is beauty subjective or objective? If you were blind, if you were deaf and could not hear any music, would you be without beauty? Or is beauty something inward? You may not see with your eyes, you may not hear with your ears; but if there is the experiencing of this state of being really open, sensitive to everything, if you are deeply aware of all that is happening inside you, of every thought, of every feeling—is there not beauty also in that? But you see, we think beauty is something outside of us.

That is why we buy pictures and hang them on the wall. We want to possess beautiful saris, suits, turbans, we want to surround ourselves with beautiful things; for we are afraid that without an objective reminder we shall lose something inwardly. But can you divide life, the whole process of existence, into the subjective and the objective? Is it not an unitary process? Without the outer there is not the inner; without the inner there is not the outer.

Questioner: Why do the strong suppress the weak?

Krishnamurti: Do you suppress the weak? Let us find out. In an argument, or in matters of physical strength, don't you push away your younger brother, the one smaller than yourself? Why? Because you want to assert yourself. You want to show your strength, you want to show how much better or more powerful you are, so you dominate, you push the little child away; you throw your weight around. It is the same with the older people. They are bigger than you are, they know a little more from reading books, they have position, money, authority, so they suppress, they push you aside; and you accept being pushed aside; and then you in your turn suppress somebody below you. Each one wants to assert himself, to dominate, to show that he has power over others. Most of us do not want to be as nothing. We want to be somebodies; and the showing of power over others gives us that satisfaction, the feeling that we *are* somebodies.

Questioner: Is that why the bigger fish swallow the smaller fish?

Krishnamurti: In the animal world it may perhaps be natural for the big fish to live on the small fish. It is something we cannot alter. But the big human being need not live on the little human being. If we know how to use our intelligence, we can stop living on each other, not only physically but also in the psychological sense. To see this problem and understand it, which is to have intelligence, is to stop living on another. But most of us *want* to live on another, so we take advantage of somebody who is weaker than ourselves. Freedom does not mean being free to do anything you like. There can be real freedom only when there is intelligence; and intelligence comes through the understanding of relationship—the relationship between you and me, and between each one of us and somebody else.

Questioner: Is it true that scientific discoveries make our lives easier to live?

Krishnamurti: Have they not made your life easier? You have electricity, have you not? You snap a switch and you have light. There is a telephone in that room, and you can talk, if you wish, to a friend in Bombay or New York. Is that not easy? Or you can take a plane and go very quickly to Delhi or to London. These things are all the outcome of scientific discoveries, and they have made life easier. Science has helped to cure diseases, but it has also given us the hydrogen bomb, which can kill thousands of human beings. So, as science is constantly discovering more and more, if we do not begin to use scientific knowledge with intelligence, with love, we are going to destroy ourselves.

Questioner: What is death?

Krishnamurti: What is death? This question from a little girl!
    You have seen dead bodies being carried to the river; you have seen dead leaves, dead trees; you know that fruits wither

and decay. The birds that are so full of life in the morning, chattering away, calling to each other, by evening may be dead. The person who is alive today may be struck down by disaster tomorrow. We see all this going on. Death is common to us all. We will all end that way. You may live for thirty, fifty, or eighty years, enjoying, suffering, being fearful; and at the end of it you are no more.

What is it that we call living, and what is it that we call death? It is really a complex problem and I do not know if you want to go into it. If we can find out, if we can understand what living is, then perhaps we shall understand what death is. When we lose someone whom we love, we feel bereft, lonely; therefore we say that death has nothing to do with living. We separate death from life. But is death separate from life? Is not living a process of dying?

For most of us, living means what? It means accumulating, choosing, suffering, laughing. And in the background, behind all the pleasure and pain, there is fear—the fear of coming to an end, the fear of what is going to happen tomorrow, the fear of being without name and fame, without property and position, all of which we want to continue. But death is inevitable; so we say, "What happens after death?"

Now, what is it that comes to an end in death? Is it life? What is life? Is life merely a process of breathing in air and expelling it? Eating, hating, loving, acquiring, possessing, comparing, being envious—this is what most of us know as life. For most of us life is suffering, a constant battle of pain and pleasure, hope and frustration. And can that not come to an end? Should we not die? In the autumn, with the coming of cold weather, the leaves fall from the trees, and reappear in the spring. Similarly, should we not die to everything of yesterday, to all our accumulations and hopes, to all the successes that we have gathered? Should we not die to all that and live again tomorrow, so that, like a new leaf, we are fresh, tender, sensitive? To a man who is constantly dying, there is no death. But the man who says, "I am somebody and I must continue"—to him there is always death and the *burning-ghat*; and that man knows no love.

14

What Is Envy?

There are various factors involved in human disintegration, and various ways in which human beings disintegrate. To integrate is to bring together, to make complete. If you are integrated, your thoughts, feelings and actions are entirely one, moving in one direction; they are not in contradiction with each other. You are a whole human being, without conflict. That is what is implied by integration. To disintegrate is the opposite of that; it is to go to pieces, to tear asunder, to scatter that which has been put together. And there are many ways in which human beings disintegrate, go to pieces, destroy themselves. I think one of the major factors is the feeling of envy, which is so subtle that it is regarded, under different names, as being worthwhile, beneficial, a creditable element in human endeavor.

Do you know what envy is? It begins when you are still very small—you feel envious of a friend who looks better than you do, who has better things or a better position. You are jealous if another boy or girl surpasses you in class, has richer parents, or belongs to a more distinguished family. So, envy or jealousy begins at a very tender age, and it gradually takes the form of competition. You want to do something to distinguish yourself—get better marks, be a better athlete than someone else; you want to outdo, to outshine others.

As you grow older, envy gets stronger and stronger. The poor envy the rich, and the rich envy the richer. There is the envy of those who have had experience and want more experience, and the envy of the writer who wants to write still better. The very desire to be better, to become something worthwhile, to have more of this or more of that, is acquisitiveness, the process of gathering, holding. If you observe you will notice that the instinct in most of us is to acquire, to get more and more saris, clothes, houses, property. If it is not that, then we want more experience, more knowledge; we want to feel that we know more than anyone else, that we have read much more than another. We want to be nearer than others to some big official high up in the government, or to feel that we are spiritually, inwardly more evolved than another. We want to be conscious that we are humble, that we are virtuous, that we can explain and others cannot.

So, the more we acquire, the greater is our disintegration. The more property, the more fame, the more experience, the more knowledge we gather, the swifter is our deterioration. From the desire to be or to acquire more, springs the universal disease of jealousy, envy. Have you not observed this in yourself, and in the older people around you? Have you not noticed how the teacher wants to be a professor, and the professor wants to be the principal? Or how your own father or mother wants more property, a bigger name?

In the struggle to acquire we become cruel. In acquisition there is no love. The acquisitive way of life is an endless battle with one's neighbor, with society, in which there is constant fear; but all this we justify, and we accept jealousy as inevitable. We think that we must be acquisitive—though we call it by a better sounding word. We call it evolution, growth, development, progress, and we say it is essential.

You see, most of us are unconscious of all this; we are unaware that we are greedy, acquisitive, that our hearts are being eaten away by envy, that our minds are deteriorating. And when for a moment we do become aware of this, we justify it, or merely say it is wrong; or we try to run away from it in various ways.

Envy is a very difficult thing to uncover or discover in oneself, because the mind is the center of envy. The mind itself is envious. The very structure of the mind is built on acquisition and envy. If you watch your own thoughts, observe the way you think, you will see that what we call thinking is generally a process of comparison: "I can explain better, I have greater knowledge, more wisdom." Thinking in terms of the 'more' is the working of the acquisitive mind; it is its way of existence. If you do not think in terms of the 'more', you will find it extremely difficult to think at all. The pursuit of the 'more' is the comparative movement of thought, which creates time—time in which to become, to be somebody; it is the process of envy, of acquisition. Thinking comparatively, the mind says, "I am *this*, and some day I shall be *that*"; "I am ugly, but I am going to be beautiful in the future." So acquisitiveness, envy, comparative thinking produce discontent, restlessness; and our reaction to that is to say we must be satisfied with our lot, we must be content with what we have. That is what the people say who are at the top of the ladder. Religions universally preach contentment.

Real contentment is not a reaction, it is not the opposite of acquisitiveness; it is something much vaster and far more significant. The man whose contentment is the opposite of acquisitiveness, of envy, is like a vegetable; inwardly he is a dead entity, as most people are. Most people are very quiet because inwardly they are dead; and they are inwardly dead because they have cultivated the opposite—the opposite of everything they actually are. Being envious, they say, "I must not be envious." You may deny the everlasting struggle of envy by wearing a loincloth and saying you are not going to acquire; but this very desire to be good, to be nonacquisitive, which is the pursuit of the opposite, is still within the field of time; it is still part of the feeling of envy, because you still want to be something. Real contentment is not like that; it is something much more creative and profound. There is no contentment when you *choose* to be content; contentment does not come that way. Contentment comes when you understand what you actually are and do not pursue what you should be.

You think you will be content when you have achieved all that you want. You may want to be a governor, or a great saint, and you think you will have contentment by achieving that end. In other words, through the process of envy you hope to arrive at contentment. Through a wrong means you expect to achieve a right result. Contentment is not satisfaction. Contentment is something very vital; it is a state of creativeness in which there is the understanding of what actually *is*. If you begin to understand what you actually are from moment to moment, from day to day, you will find that out of this understanding there comes an extraordinary feeling of vastness, of limitless comprehension. That is, if you are greedy, what matters is to understand your greed and not try to become non-greedy; because the very desire to become non-greedy is still a form of greed.

Our religious structure, our ways of thinking, our social life, everything we do is based on acquisitiveness, on an envious outlook, and for centuries we have been brought up like that. We are so conditioned to it that we cannot think apart from the 'better', the 'more'; therefore we make envy desirable. We do not call it envy, we call it by some euphemistic term; but if you go behind the word you will see that this extraordinary desire for the 'more' is egocentric, self-enclosing. It is limiting thought.

The mind that is limited by envy, by the 'me', by the acquisitive desire for things or for virtue, can never be a truly religious mind. The religious mind is not a comparative mind. The religious mind sees and understands the full significance of *what is*. That is why it is very important to understand yourself, which is to perceive the workings of your own mind: the motives, the intentions, the longings, the desires, the constant pressure of pursuance which creates envy, acquisitiveness, and comparison. When all these have come to an end through the understanding of *what is*, only then will you know true religion, what God is.

Questioner: Is truth relative or absolute?

Krishnamurti: First of all, let us look through the words at the significance of the question. We want something absolute, don't we? The human craving is for something permanent, fixed, immovable, eternal, something that does not decay, that has no death—an idea, a feeling, a state that is everlasting, so that the mind can cling to it. We must understand this craving before we can understand the question and answer it rightly.

The human mind wants permanency in everything—in relationship, in property, in virtue. It wants something which cannot be destroyed. That is why we say God is permanent, or truth is absolute.

But what is truth? Is truth some extraordinary mystery, something far away, unimaginable, abstract? Or is truth something which you discover from moment to moment, from day to day? If it can be accumulated, gathered through experience, then it is not truth; for behind this gathering lies the same spirit of acquisitiveness. If it is something far away which can be found only through a system of meditation, or through the practice of denial and sacrifice, again it is not truth for that also is a process of acquisitiveness.

Truth is to be discovered and understood in every action, in every thought, in every feeling, however trivial or transient; it is to be observed at each moment of every day; it is to be listened to in what the husband and the wife say, in what the gardener says, in what your friends say, and in the process of your own thinking. Your thinking may be false, it may be conditioned, limited; and to discover that your thinking is conditioned, limited, is truth. That very discovery sets your mind free from limitation. If you discover that you are greedy—if you *discover* it, and are not just told by somebody else—that discovery is truth, and that truth has its own action upon your greed.

Truth is not something which you can gather, accumulate, store up and then rely on as a guide. That is only another form of possession. And it is very difficult for the mind not to acquire, not to store up. When you realize the significance of this, you will find out what an extraordinary thing truth is. Truth is timeless, but the moment you capture it—as when you say, "I have found truth, it is mine"—it is no longer truth.

So, whether truth is "absolute" or timeless depends on the mind. When the mind says, "I want the absolute, something which never decays, which knows no death," what it really wants is something permanent to cling to; so it creates the permanent. But in a mind that is aware of everything that is happening outwardly and within itself, and sees the truth of it—such a mind is timeless; and only such a mind can know that which is beyond names, beyond the permanent and the impermanent.

Questioner: What is external awareness?

Krishnamurti: Are you not aware that you are sitting in this hall? Are you not aware of the trees, of the sunshine? Are you not aware that the crow is cawing, the dog is barking? Do you not see the color of the flowers, the movement of the leaves, the people walking by? That is external awareness. When you see the sunset, the stars at night, the moonlight on the water, all that is external awareness, is it not? And as you are externally aware, so also you can be inwardly aware of your thoughts and feelings, of your motives and urges, of your prejudices, envies, greed, and pride. If you are really aware outwardly, the inward awareness also begins to awaken, and you become more and more conscious of your reaction to what people say, to what you read, and so on. The external reaction or response in your relationship with other people is the outcome of an inward state of wanting, of hope, of anxiety, fear. This outward and inward awareness is an unitary process which brings about a total integration of human understanding.

Questioner: What is real and eternal happiness?

Krishnamurti: When you are completely healthy, you are not conscious of your body, are you? It is only when there is disease, discomfort, pain, that you become conscious of it. When you are free to think completely, without resistance, there is no consciousness of thinking. It is only when there is friction, a blockage, a limitation, that you begin to be conscious of a thinker. Similarly, is happiness something of which you are aware? In the moment of joy, are you aware that you are joyous? It is only when you are unhappy that you want happiness; and then this question arises, "What is real and eternal happiness?"

You see how the mind plays tricks on itself. Because you are unhappy, miserable, in poor circumstances, and so on, you want something eternal, a permanent happiness. And is there such a thing? Instead of asking about permanent happiness, find out how to be free of the diseases which are gnawing at you and creating pain, both physical and psychological. When you are free, there is no problem, you don't ask whether there is eternal happiness or what that happiness is. It is a lazy, foolish man who, being in prison, wants to know what freedom is; and lazy, foolish people will tell him. To the man in prison, freedom is mere speculation. But if he gets out of that prison, he does not speculate about freedom: it is there.

So, is it not important, instead of asking what happiness is, to find out why we are unhappy? Why is the mind crippled? Why is it that our thoughts are limited, small, petty? If we can understand the limitation of thought, see the truth of it, in that discovery of the truth there is liberation.

Questioner: Why do people want things?

Krishnamurti: Don't you want food when you are hungry? Don't you want clothes and a house to shelter you? These are normal wants, are they not? Healthy people naturally recognize that they need certain things. It is only the diseased or unbalanced man who says, "I do not need food." It is a perverted mind that must either have many houses, or no house at all to live in.

Your body gets hungry because you are using energy, so it wants more food; that is normal. But if you say, "I must have the tastiest food, I must have only the food that my tongue takes pleasure in," then perversion begins. All of us—not only the rich, but everybody in the world—must have food, clothing, and shelter; but if these physical necessities are limited, controlled, and made available only to the few, then there is perversion; an unnatural process is set going. If you say, "I must accumulate, I must have everything for myself," you are depriving others of that which is essential for their daily needs.

You see, the problem is not simple, because we want other things besides what is essential for our daily needs. I may be satisfied with a little food, a few clothes, and a small room to live in; but I want something else. I want to be a well-known person, I want position, power, prestige, I want to be nearest to God, I want my friends to think well of me, and so on. These inward wants pervert the outward interests of every human being. The problem is a little difficult because the inward desire to be the richest or most powerful man, the urge to be somebody, is dependent for its fulfillment on the possession of things, including food, clothing, and shelter. I lean on these things in order to become inwardly rich; but as long as I am in this state of dependence, it is impossible for me to be inwardly rich, which is to be utterly simple inwardly.

15

It Is Understanding That Is Creative, Not Memory

*P*erhaps some of you are interested in what I have been saying about envy. I am not using the word *remember* because, as I have explained, merely to remember words or phrases makes the mind dull, lethargic, heavy, uncreative. It is very destructive merely to remember. What is important, especially while you are young, is to understand rather than to cultivate memory; because understanding frees the mind, it awakens the critical faculty of analysis. It enables you to see the significance of the fact and not just rationalize it. When you merely remember certain phrases, sentences, or ideas about envy for example, that remembrance prevents you from looking at the fact of envy. But if you see and understand the envy which lurks behind the facade of good works, of philanthropy, of religion, and behind your own desire to be great, to be saintly—if you really see and understand this for yourself, then you will discover what an extraordinary freedom there is from envy, from jealousy.

So it is really important to understand, because remembrance is a dead thing; and perhaps that is one of the major causes of human deterioration. We are very inclined to imitate, to copy, to follow ideals, heroes; and what happens? Gradually the flame of creativity is lost and only the picture, the symbol, the word remains, without anything behind it. We are taught to memorize, and this is obviously not creative. There is no understanding in merely remembering things that you have read in books, or that you have been taught; and when throughout life memory alone is cultivated, real understanding is gradually destroyed.

Please listen carefully, because it is very important to understand this. It is *understanding* that is creative, not memory, not remembrance. Understanding is the liberating factor, not the things you have stored up in your mind. And understanding is not in the future. The mere cultivation of memory brings about the idea of the future; but if you understand directly, that is, if you see something very clearly for yourself, then there is no problem. A problem exists only when you do not see clearly.

What is important, then, is not what you know, not the knowledge or the experience you have gathered, but to see things as they are and to understand them immediately; because comprehension is immediate, it is not in the future. When experience and knowledge take the place of understanding, they become deteriorating factors in life. For most of us, knowledge and experience are very important; but if you go behind the words and see the real significance of knowledge and experience, you will find that they become major factors in human deterioration. This does not mean that knowledge is not right at certain levels of our existence. It is right and necessary to know how to plant a tree and what kind of nourishment it should have, or how to feed the chickens, or how to raise a family properly, or how to build a bridge, and so on. There is an enormous amount of scientific knowledge available, which can be used rightly. It is right, for example, that we should know how to build a dynamo or a motor. But when there is no understanding, then knowledge, which is merely memory, becomes very destructive; and you will find that experience also becomes destructive, because experience strengthens the background of memory.

I wonder if you have noticed how many grown-up people think bureaucratically, as officials. If they are teachers, their thinking is limited to that function; they are not human beings pulsating with life. They know the rules of grammar, or mathematics, or a little history; and because their thinking is circumscribed by that memory, that experience, their knowledge is destroying them. Life is not a thing that you learn from somebody. Life is something that you listen to, that you understand from moment to moment without accumulating experience. After all, what have you got when you have accumulated experience? When you say, "I have had an enormous amount of experience," or "I know the meaning of those words," it is memory, is it not? You have had certain experiences, you have learned how to run an office, how to put up a building or a bridge, and according to that background you get further experience. You cultivate experience, which is memory; and with that memory you meet life.

Like the river, life is running, swift, volatile, never still; and when you meet life with the heavy burden of memory, naturally you are never in contact with life. You are meeting life with your own knowledge, experience, which only increases the burden of memory; so knowledge and experience gradually become destructive factors in life.

I hope you are understanding this very deeply, because what I am saying is very true; and if you understand it, you will use knowledge at its proper level. But if you do not understand and merely accumulate knowledge and experience as a means to get on in life, as a means to strengthen your position in the world, then knowledge and experience will become most destructive, they will destroy your initiative, your creativeness. Most of us are so burdened with authority, with what other people have said, with the Bhagavad Gita, with ideas, that our lives have become very dull. These are all memories, remembrances; they are not things that we have understood, they are not living. There is no new thing as long as we are burdened with memories; and life being everlastingly new, we cannot understand it. Therefore our living is very tedious; we become lethargic, we grow mentally and physically fat and ugly. It is very important to understand this.

Simplicity is freedom of the mind from experience, from the burden of memory. We think that simplicity is a matter of having but few clothes and a begging bowl; we think that a simple life consists in possessing very little externally. That may be all right. But real simplicity is freedom from knowledge, freedom from remembering or accumulating experience. Have you not noticed the people who make a point of having very little and who think they are very simple? Have you not listened to them? Though they may have only a loincloth and a staff, they are full of ideals. Inwardly they are very complex, battling against themselves, struggling to follow their own projections, their own beliefs. Inwardly they are not simple; they are full of what they have gathered from books, full of ideals, dogmas, fears. Outwardly they may have only a staff and a few clothes. But real simplicity of life is to be inwardly empty, innocent, without the accumulation of knowledge, without beliefs, dogmas, without the fear of authority; and that state of inward simplicity can come into being only when you really understand every experience from moment to moment. If you have understood an experience, then that experience is over, it leaves no residue. It is because we do not understand experience, because we remember the pleasure or the pain of it, that we are never inwardly simple. Those who are religiously inclined pursue the things that make for outward simplicity; but inwardly they are chaotic, confused, burdened with innumerable longings, desires, knowledge; they are frightened of living, of experiencing.

If you look at envy, you will see that it is a deep-rooted form of remembering which is a very destructive, a very deteriorating factor in our lives; and so likewise is experience. This does not mean that you must forget everyday facts, or avoid experience. You can't. But the man who is full of experience is not necessarily a wise man. The man who has an experience and just clings to that experience is not a wise man; he is like any schoolboy who reads and accumulates information from books. A wise man is innocent, free of experience; he is inwardly simple, though outwardly he may have all the things of the earth—or very little.

Questioner: Does intelligence build character?

Krishnamurti: What do we mean by *character*? And what do we mean by *intelligence*? Every politician—whether the Delhi variety, or your own local tub-thumper—continually uses such words as *character, ideal, intelligence, religion, God*. We listen to these words with rapt attention, because they seem very important. Most of us live on words; and the more elaborate, the more exquisite the words, the more satisfied we feel. So, let us find out what we mean by *intelligence* and what we mean by *character*. Don't say I am not answering you definitely. To seek definitions, conclusions, is one of the tricks of the mind, and it means that you don't want to investigate and understand, you just want to follow words.

What is intelligence? If a man is frightened, anxious, envious, greedy; if his mind is copying, imitating, filled with other people's experiences and knowledge; if his thinking is limited, shaped by society, by environment—is such a man intelligent? He is not, is he? And can a man who is frightened, unintelligent, have character—character being something original, not the mere repeating of traditional *do's* and *don'ts?* Is character respectability?

Do you understand what that word *respectability* means? You are respectable when you are looked up to, respected by a majority of the people around you. And what do the majority of people respect—the people of the family, the people of the mass? They respect the things which they themselves want and which they have projected as a goal or an ideal; they respect that which they see to be in contrast with their own more lowly state. If you are rich and powerful, or have a big name politically, or have written successful books, you are respected by the majority. What you say may be utter nonsense, but when you talk, people listen because they regard you as a great man. And when you have thus won the respect of the many, the following of the multitude, it gives you a sense of respectability, a feeling of having arrived. But the so-called sinner is nearer to God than the respectable man, because the respectable man is clothed in hypocrisy.

Is character the outcome of imitation, of being controlled by the fear of what people will say or won't say? Is character the mere strengthening of one's own tendencies, prejudices? Is it an upholding of the tradition, whether of India, of Europe or America? That is generally called having character—being a strong person who supports the local tradition and so is respected by the many. But when you are prejudiced, imitative, bound by tradition, or when you are frightened, is there intelligence, is there character? Imitating, following, worshipping, having ideals—that way leads to respectability, but not to understanding. A man of ideals is respectable; but he will never be near God, he will never know what it is to love, because his ideals are a means of covering up his fear, his imitation, his loneliness.

So, without understanding yourself, without being aware of all that is operating in your own mind—how you think, whether you are copying, imitating, whether you are frightened, whether you are seeking power—there cannot be intelligence. And it is intelligence that creates character, not hero worship or the pursuit of an ideal. The understanding of oneself, of one's own extraordinarily complicated self, is the beginning of intelligence, which reveals character.

Questioner: Why does a man feel disturbed when another person looks at him intently?

Krishnamurti: Do you feel nervous when someone looks at you? When a servant, a villager—someone whom you consider inferior—looks at you, you do not even know he is there, you just pass him by; you have no regard for him. But when your father, your mother, or your teacher looks at you, you feel somewhat anxious because they know more than you do, and they may find out things about you. Going a little higher, if a government official or some other prominent visitor takes notice of you, you are pleased, because you hope to get something from him, a job or some kind of reward. And if a man looks at you from whom you do not want anything, you are quite indifferent, are you not? So it is important to find out what is operating in your own mind when people look at you, because how you inwardly respond to a look or a smile means a great deal.

Unfortunately, most of us are utterly unaware of all these things. We never notice the beggar, or the villager carrying his heavy burden, or the flying parrot. We are so occupied with our own sorrows, longings, fears, with our pleasures and rituals that we are unaware of many significant things in life.

Questioner: Can we not cultivate understanding? When we constantly try to understand, does it not mean that we are practicing understanding?

Krishnamurti: Is understanding cultivable? Is it something to be practiced as you practice tennis, or the piano, or singing, or dancing? You can read a book over and over again till you are thoroughly familiar with it. Is understanding like that, something to be learned through constant repetition, which is really the cultivation of memory? Is not understanding from moment to moment, and therefore something that cannot be practiced?

When do you understand? What is the state of your mind and heart when there is understanding? When you hear me say something very true about jealousy—that jealousy is destructive, that envy is a major factor in the deterioration of human relationship—how do you respond to it? Do you see the truth of it immediately? Or do you begin to think about jealousy, to talk about it, rationalize it, analyze it? Is understanding a process of either rationalization or slow analysis? Can understanding be cultivated as you cultivate your garden to produce fruits or flowers? Surely, to understand is to see the truth of something directly, without any barrier of words, prejudices or motives.

Questioner: Is the power of understanding the same in all persons?

Krishnamurti: Suppose something true is presented to you and you see the truth of it very quickly; your understanding is immediate because you have no barriers. You are not full of your own importance, you are eager to find out, so you perceive immediately. But I have many barriers, many prejudices. I am jealous, torn by conflicts based upon envy, full of my own importance. I have accumulated many things in life, and I really do not *want* to see; therefore I do not see, I do not understand.

Questioner: Can't one remove the barriers slowly by constantly trying to understand?

Krishnamurti: No. I can remove the barriers, not by trying to understand, but only when I really feel the importance of not having barriers—which means that I must be willing to see the barriers. Suppose you and I hear someone say that envy is destructive. You listen and understand the significance, the truth of it, and you are free of that feeling of envy, of jealousy. But I do not want to see the truth of it, because if I did it would destroy my whole structure of life.

Questioner: I feel the necessity of removing the barriers.

Krishnamurti: Why do you feel that? Do you want to remove the barriers because of circumstances? Do you want to remove them because somebody has told you that you should? Surely, the barriers are removed only when you see for yourself that to have barriers of any kind creates a mind which is in a state of slow decay. And when do you see this? When you suffer? But does suffering necessarily awaken you to the importance of removing all barriers? Or does it, on the contrary, lead you to create more barriers?

You will find that all barriers drop away when you yourself are beginning to listen, to observe, to find out. There is no reason for removing the barriers; and the moment you bring in a reason, you are not removing them. The miracle, the greatest blessing is to give your own inward perception an opportunity to remove the barriers. But when you say that the barriers must be removed and then practice removing them, that is the work of the mind; and the mind cannot remove the barriers. You must see that no attempt on your part can remove them. Then the mind becomes very quiet, very still; and in this stillness you discover that which is true.

16

Understanding the Significance of Words

We have been talking about the deteriorating factors in human existence, and we said that fear is one of the fundamental causes of this deterioration. We also said that the following of authority in any form, whether self-imposed or established from outside, as well as any form of imitation, copying, is destructive of incentive, of creativeness, and that it blocks the discovery of what is true.

Truth is not something that can be followed; it has to be discovered. You cannot find truth through any book or through any accumulation of experience. As we discussed the other day, when experience becomes a remembrance, that remembrance destroys creative understanding. Any feeling of malice or envy, however slight it may be, is also destructive of this creative understanding without which there is no happiness. Happiness is not to be bought, nor does it come when you go after it; but it is there when there is no conflict.

Now, is it not very important, especially while we are still in school, to begin to understand the significance of words? The word, the symbol has become an extraordinarily destructive thing for most of us, and of this we are unaware. Do you know what I mean by the symbol? The symbol is the shadow of truth. The gramophone record, for example, is not the real voice; but the voice has been put on the record, and to this we listen. The word, the symbol, the image, the idea is not the truth; but we worship the image, we revere the symbol, we give great significance to the word, and all this is very destructive; because then the word, the symbol, the image becomes all-important. That is how temples, churches, and the various organized religions with their symbols, beliefs, and dogmas become factors which prevent the mind from going beyond and discovering the truth. So do not be caught up in words, in symbols, which automatically cultivate habit. Habit is a most destructive factor, because when you want to think creatively, habit comes in the way.

Perhaps you do not understand the whole significance of what I am saying, but you will if you think about it. Go for a walk by yourself occasionally and think out these things. Find out what is meant by words like *life, God, duty, cooperation*—all those extraordinary words which we use so freely.

Have you ever asked yourself what *duty* means? Duty to what? To the aged, to what tradition says: that you must sacrifice yourself for your parents, for your country, for your gods. That word *duty* has become extraordinarily significant to you, has it not? It is pregnant with a lot of meaning which is imposed upon you. You are taught that you have a duty to your country, to your gods, to your neighbor; but what is much more important than the word *duty* is to find out for yourself what the truth is. Your parents and society use that word *duty* as a means of molding you, shaping you according to their particular idiosyncrasies, their habits of thought, their likes and dislikes, hoping thereby to guarantee their own safety. So take time, be patient, analyze, go into all this and find out for yourself what is true. Do not merely accept the word *duty*, for where there is 'duty', there is no love.

Similarly, take the word *cooperation*. The state wants you to cooperate with it. If you cooperate with something without understanding, you are merely imitating, copying. But if you understand, if you find out the truth of something, then in cooperating you are living with it, moving with it; it is part of you.

So it is very necessary to be aware of the words, the symbols, the images that are crippling your thinking. To be aware of them and to find out whether you can go beyond them is essential if you are to live creatively, without disintegrating.

You know, we allow the word *duty* to kill us. The idea that you have a duty to parents, to relations, to the country, sacrifices you. It makes you go out to fight, to kill, and to be killed or maimed. The politician, the leader says it is necessary to destroy others in order to protect the community, the country, the ideology or way of life; so killing becomes part of your duty, and you are soon drawn into the military spirit. The military spirit makes you obedient, it makes you physically very disciplined; but inwardly your mind is gradually destroyed because you are imitating, following, copying. You become a mere tool of the older people, of the politician, an instrument of propaganda. You come to accept killing to protect your country as inevitable because somebody says it is necessary. But no matter *who* says it is necessary, should you not think it out very clearly for yourself?

To kill is obviously the most destructive and corrupt action in life, especially to kill another human being; because when you kill, you are full of hatred, however much you may rationalize it, and you also create antagonism in others. You can kill with a word as well as with an action; and killing other human beings has never solved any of our problems. War has never cured any of our economic or social ills, nor has it brought about mutual understanding in human relationship; and yet the whole world is everlastingly preparing for war. Many reasons are put forward as to why it is necessary to kill people; and there are also many reasons for not killing. But do not be swept away by any reasoning; because today you may have a good reason for not killing and tomorrow you may have a much stronger reason for killing.

First see the truth of it, feel how essential it is not to kill. Regardless of what may be said by others, from the highest authority to the lowest, find out for yourself the truth of the matter; and when you are inwardly clear about that, then you can reason out the details. But do not start with a reason, because every reason can be met by a counter-reason and you will be caught in the net of reasoning. The important thing is to see directly for yourself what the truth is; and then you can begin to use reason. When you perceive for yourself what is true; when you know that to kill another is not love; when you inwardly feel the truth that there must be no enmity in your relationship with another, then no amount of reasoning can destroy that truth. Then no politician, no priest, no parent can sacrifice you for an idea or for his own safety.

The old have always sacrificed the young; and will you in your turn, as you grow older, also sacrifice the young? Do you not want to put an end to this sacrifice? Because it is the most destructive way of living, it is one of the greatest factors of human deterioration. To put an end to it, you as an individual have to find out the truth for yourself. Without belonging to any group or organization, you have to discover the truth of not killing, of feeling love, of having no enmity. Then no amount of words, no cunning reasons can ever persuade you to kill or to sacrifice another.

So it is very important, while you are young, to think out,

to feel out these things for yourself, and thereby lay the foundation for the discovery of truth.

Questioner: What is the purpose of creation?

Krishnamurti: Are you really interested in that? What do you mean by *creation?* What is the purpose of living? Why do you exist, read, study, pass examinations? What is the purpose of relationship—the relationship of parents and children, of husband and wife? What is life? Is that what you mean when you ask this question, "What is the purpose of creation?" When do you ask such a question? When inwardly you do not see clearly, when you are confused, miserable, in the dark, when you do not perceive or feel the truth of the matter for yourself, then you want to know what is the purpose of life.

Now, there are many people who will tell you the purpose of life; they will tell you what the sacred books say. Clever people will go on inventing various purposes of life. The political group will have one purpose, the religious group will have another, and so on and on. And how are you to find out what is the purpose of life when you yourself are confused? Surely, as long as you are confused, you can only receive an answer which is also confused. If your mind is disturbed, if it is not really quiet, whatever answer you receive will be through this screen of confusion, anxiety, fear; therefore the answer will be perverted. So the important thing is not to ask what is the purpose of life, but to clear away the confusion that is within you. It is like a blind man asking, "What is light?" If I try to tell him what light is, he will listen according to his blindness, according to his darkness; but from the moment he is able to see, he will never ask what is light. It is there.

Similarly, if you can clarify the confusion within yourself, then you will find out what the purpose of life is; you will not have to ask, you will not have to look for it. To be free of confusion you have to see and understand the causes which bring about confusion; and the causes of confusion are very clear. They are rooted in the 'me' that is constantly wanting to expand itself through possessing, through becoming, through success, through imitation; and the symptoms are jealousy, envy, greed, fear. As long as there is this inward confusion, you are always seeking outward answers; but when the inward confusion is cleared away, then you will know the significance of life.

Questioner: What is karma?

Krishnamurti: Karma is one of the peculiar words we use, it is one of those words in which our thought is caught. The poor man has to accept life in terms of a theory. He has to accept misery, starvation, squalor, because he is underfed and has not the energy to break away and create a revolution. He has to accept what life gives him, and so he says, "It is my karma to be like this"; and the politicians, the big ones, encourage him to accept his misery. You do not want him to revolt against all this, do you? But when you pay the poor man so little while you have so much, that is very likely to happen; so you use that word *karma* to encourage his passive acceptance of the misery in his life.

The educated man, the man who has achieved, who has inherited, who has come to the top of things, the man who has power, position, and the means of corruption—he also says, "It is my karma. I have done well in a previous life and now I am reaping the reward of my past action."

But is that the meaning of karma—to accept things as they

are? Do you understand? Does karma mean accepting things as they are without question, without a spark of revolt—which is the attitude many of us have? So you see how easily certain words become a net in which we get caught, because we are not really alive. The true significance of that word *karma* cannot be understood as a theory; it cannot be understood if you say, "That is what the Bhagavad Gita says."

You know, the comparative mind is the most stupid mind of all, because it does not think; it merely says, "I have read such-and-such a book, and what you say is like it." When you say this, you have stopped thinking; when you compare, you are no longer investigating to find out what is true, irrespective of what any particular book or guru has said. So, what is important is to throw off all authorities and investigate, find out, and not compare. Comparison is the worship of authority, it is imitation, thoughtlessness. To compare is the very nature of a mind that is not awake to discover what is true. You say, "That is so, it is like what was said by the Buddha," and you think you have thereby solved your problems. But really to discover the truth of anything, you have to be extremely active, vigorous, self-reliant; and you cannot have self-reliance as long as you are thinking comparatively. Please listen to this. If there is no self-reliance, you lose all power to investigate and find out what is true. Self-reliance brings a certain freedom in which you discover; and that freedom is denied to you when you are comparing.

Questioner: Is there an element of fear in respect?

Krishnamurti: What do *you* say? When you show respect to your teacher, to your parents, to your guru, and disrespect to your servant; when you kick the people who are not important to you, and lick the boots of those who are above you, the officials, the politicians, the big ones—is there not an element of fear in this? From the big ones, from the teacher, the examiner, the professor, from your parents, from the politician or the bank manager, you hope to get something; therefore you are respectful. But what can the poor people give you? So the poor you disregard, you treat them with contempt, you do not even know they are there when they pass you in the street. You do not look at them, it does not concern you that they shiver in the cold, that they are dirty and hungry. But you will give to the big ones, to the great of the land, even when you have very little, in order to receive more of their favors. In this there is definitely an element of fear, is there not? There is no love. If you had love in your heart, you would show respect to those who have nothing and also to those who have everything; you would neither be afraid of those who have, nor disregard those who have not. Respect in the hope of reward is the outcome of fear. In love there is no fear.

17

Can the Mind Ever Find Peace?

We have been examining the various factors that bring about deterioration in our lives, in our activities, in our thoughts; and we have seen that conflict is one of the major factors of this deterioration. And is not peace also, as it is generally understood, a destructive factor? Can peace be brought about by the mind? If we have peace through the mind, does not that also lead to corruption, deterioration? If we are not very alert and observant, that word *peace* becomes like a narrow window through which we look at the world and try to understand it. Through a narrow window we can see only part of the sky, and not the whole vastness, the magnificence of it. There is no possibility of having peace by merely pursuing peace, which is inevitably a process of the mind.

It may be a little difficult to understand this, but I shall try to make it as simple and clear as I can. If we can understand what it means to be peaceful, then perhaps we shall understand the real significance of love.

We think that peace is something to be achieved through the mind, through reason, but is it? Can peace ever come about through any quieting, through any control or domination of thought? We all want peace; and for most of us, peace means to be left alone, not to be disturbed or interfered with, so we build a wall around our own mind, a wall of ideas.

It is very important for you to understand this, for as you grow older you will be faced with the problems of war and peace. Is peace something to be pursued, caught, and tamed by the mind? What most of us call peace is a process of stagnation, a slow decay. We think we shall find peace by clinging to a set of ideas, by inwardly building a wall of security, safety, a wall of habits, beliefs; we think that peace is a matter of pursuing a principle, of cultivating a particular tendency, a particular fancy, a particular wish. We want to live without disturbance, so we find some corner of the universe, or of our own being, into which we crawl, and we live in the darkness of self-enclosure. That is what most of us seek in our relationship with the husband, with the wife, with parents, with friends. Unconsciously we want peace at any price, and so we pursue it.

But can the mind ever find peace? Is not the mind itself a source of disturbance? The mind can only gather, accumulate, deny, assert, remember, pursue. Peace is absolutely essential, because without peace we cannot live creatively. But is peace something to be realized through the struggles, the denials, the sacrifices of the mind? Do you understand what I am talking about?

We may be discontented while we are young, but as we grow older, unless we are very wise and watchful, that discontent will be canalized into some form of peaceful resignation to life. The mind is everlastingly seeking a secluded habit, belief, desire, something in which it can live and be at peace with the world. But the mind cannot find peace, because it can think only in terms of time, in terms of the past, the present and the future:

what it has been, what it is, and what it will be. It is constantly condemning, judging, weighing, comparing, pursuing its own vanities, its own habits, beliefs; and such a mind can never be peaceful. It can delude itself into a state which it calls peace; but that is not peace. The mind can mesmerize itself by the repetition of words and phrases, by following somebody, or by accumulating knowledge; but it is not peaceful, because such a mind is itself the center of disturbance, it is by its very nature the essence of time. So the mind with which we think, with which we calculate, with which we contrive and compare, is incapable of finding peace.

Peace is not the outcome of reason; and yet, as you will see if you observe them, the organized religions are caught up in this pursuit of peace through the mind. Real peace is as creative and as pure as war is destructive; and to find that peace, one must understand beauty. That is why it is important, while we are very young, to have beauty about us—the beauty of buildings that have proper proportions, the beauty of cleanliness, of quiet talk among the elders. In understanding what beauty is, we shall know love, for the understanding of beauty is the peace of the heart.

Peace is of the heart, not of the mind. To know peace you have to find out what beauty is. The way you talk, the words you use, the gestures you make—these things matter very much, for through them you will discover the refinement of your own heart. Beauty cannot be defined, it cannot be explained in words. It can be understood only when the mind is very quiet.

So, while you are young and sensitive, it is essential that you—as well as those who are responsible for you—should create an atmosphere of beauty. The way you dress, the way you walk, the way you sit, the way you eat—all these things, and the things about you, are very important. As you grow up you will meet the ugly things of life—ugly buildings, ugly people with their malice, envy, ambition, cruelty; and if in your heart there is not founded and established the perception of beauty, you will easily be swept away by the enormous current of the world. Then you will get caught in the endless struggle to find peace through the mind. The mind projects an idea of what peace is and tries to pursue it, thereby getting caught in the net of words, in the net of fancies and illusions.

Peace can come only when there is love. If you have peace merely through security, financial or otherwise, or through certain dogmas, rituals, verbal repetitions, there is no creativeness; there is no urgency to bring about a fundamental revolution in the world. Such peace only leads to contentment and resignation. But when in you there is the understanding of love and beauty, then you will find the peace that is not a mere projection of the mind. It is this peace that is creative, that removes confusion and brings order within oneself. But this peace does not come through any effort to find it. It comes when you are constantly watching, when you are sensitive to both the ugly and the beautiful, to the good and the bad, to all the fluctuations of life. Peace is not something petty, created by the mind; it is enormously great, infinitely extensive, and it can be understood only when the heart is full.

Questioner: Why do we feel inferior before our superiors?

Krishnamurti: Whom do you consider your superiors? Those who know? Those who have titles, degrees? Those from whom you want something, some kind of reward or position? The moment you regard somebody as superior, do you not regard somebody else as inferior?

Why do we have this division of the superior and the inferior? It exists only when we want something, does it not? I feel less intelligent than you are, I do not have as much money or capacity as you have, I am not as happy as you seem to be, or I want something from you; so I feel inferior to you. When I am envious of you, or when I am trying to imitate you, or when I want something from you, I immediately become your inferior, because I have put you on a pedestal, I have given you a superior value. So, psychologically, inwardly, I create both the superior and the inferior; I create this sense of inequality between those who have and those who have not.

Among human beings there is enormous inequality of capacity, is there not? There is the man who designs the jet plane, and the man who guides the plough. These vast differences in capacity—intellectual, verbal, physical—are inevitable. But, you see, we give tremendous significance to certain functions. We consider the governor, the prime minister, the inventor, the scientist as being enormously more important than the servant; so function assumes status. As long as we give status to particular functions, there is bound to be a sense of inequality, and the gap between those who are capable and those who are not becomes unbridgeable. If we can keep function stripped of status, then there is a possibility of bringing about a real feeling of equality. But for this there must be love; because it is love that destroys the sense of the inferior and the superior.

The world is divided into those who have—the rich, the powerful, the capable, those who have everything—and those who have not. And is it possible to bring about a world in which this division between the haves and the have-nots does not exist? Actually, what is happening is this: seeing the breach, this gulf between the rich and the poor, between the man of great capacity and the man of little or no capacity, the politicians and economists are trying to solve the problem through economic and social reform. That may be all right. But a real transformation can never take place as long as we do not understand the whole process of antagonism, envy, malice; for it is only when this process is understood and comes to an end that there can be love in our hearts.

Questioner: Is it possible to have peace in our lives when at every moment we are struggling against our environment?

Krishnamurti: What is our environment? Our environment is society, the economic, religious, national, and class environment of the country in which we grow up; and also the climate. Most of us are struggling to fit in, to adjust ourselves to our environment, because we hope to get a job from that environment, we hope to have the benefits of that particular society. But what is that society made up of? Have you ever thought about it? Have you ever looked closely at the society in which you are living and to which you are trying to adjust yourself? That society is based on a set of beliefs and traditions which is called religion, and on certain economic values, is it not? You are part of that society, and you are struggling to adjust yourself to it. But that society is the outcome of acquisitiveness, it is the outcome of envy, fear, greed, possessive pursuits, with occasional flashes of love. And if you want to be intelligent, fearless, nonacquisitive, can you adjust yourself to such a society? Can you?

Surely, you have to create a new society, which means that you as an individual have to be free of acquisitiveness, of envy, of greed; you have to be free of nationalism, of patriotism, and of all narrowing down of religious thought. Only then is there a possibility of creating something new, a totally new society. But as long as you thoughtlessly struggle to adjust yourself to the present society, you are merely following the old pattern of envy, of power and prestige, of beliefs which are corruptive.

So it is very important, while you are young, to begin to understand these problems and bring about real freedom within yourself, for then you will create a new world, a new society, a new relationship between man and man. And to help you do this is surely the true function of education.

Questioner: Why do we suffer? Why can we not be free of disease and death?

Krishnamurti: Through sanitation, through proper living conditions and nutritious food, man is beginning to free himself from certain diseases. Through surgery and various forms of treatment, medical science is trying to find a cure for incurable diseases like cancer. A capable doctor does all he can to relieve and eliminate disease.

And is death conquerable? It is a most extraordinary thing that, at your age, you are so interested in death. Why are you so preoccupied with it? Is it because you see so much of death about you—the burning-*ghats*, the body being carried to the river? To you, death is a familiar sight, it is so constantly with you; and there is the fear of death.

If you do not reflect and understand for yourself the implications of death, you will go endlessly from one preacher to another, from one hope to another, from one belief to another, trying to find a solution to this problem of death. Do you understand? Don't keep on asking somebody else, but try to find out for yourself the truth of the matter. To ask innumerable questions without ever trying to find out or discover is characteristic of a petty mind.

You see, we fear death only when we cling to life. The understanding of the whole process of living is also the understanding of the significance of dying. Death is merely the extinction of continuity, and we are afraid of not being able to continue; but what continues can never be creative. Think it out; discover for yourself what is true. It is truth that liberates you from the fear of death, and not your religious theories, nor your belief in reincarnation or in life hereafter.

18

What Is Life All About?

While we are quite young, most of us are perhaps not greatly affected by the conflicts of life, by the worries, the passing joys, the physical disasters, the fear of death, and the mental twists that burden the older generation. Fortunately, while we are young most of us are not yet on the battlefield of life. But as we grow older the problems, the miseries, the doubts, the economic and inward struggles all begin to crowd in on us, and then we want to find out the significance of life, we want to know what life is all about. We wonder about the conflicts, the pains, the poverty, the disasters. We want to know why some people are well placed and others are not; why one human being is healthy, intelligent, gifted, capable, while another is not. And if we are easily satisfied, we soon get caught in some hypothesis, in some theory or belief; we find an answer, but it is never the true answer. We realize that life is ugly, painful, sorrowful, and we start out with an inquiry; but not having enough self-reliance, vigor, intelligence, innocence to go on inquiring, we are soon caught in theories, in beliefs, in some kind of speculation or doctrine which satisfactorily explains all this. Gradually our beliefs and dogmas become deep rooted and unshakable, because behind them there is a constant fear of the unknown. We never look at that fear; we turn away from it and take refuge in our beliefs. And when we examine these beliefs—the Hindu, the Buddhist, the Christian—we find that they divide people. Each set of dogmas and beliefs has a series of rituals, a series of compulsions which bind the mind and separate man from man.

So we start with an inquiry to find out what is true, what is the significance of all this misery, this struggle, this pain, and we end up with a set of beliefs, rituals, theories. We have not the self-reliance, nor the vigor, nor the innocence to push belief aside and inquire; therefore belief begins to act as a deteriorating factor in our lives.

Belief is corruptive, because behind belief and idealistic morality lurks the 'me', the self—the self which is constantly growing bigger, more powerful. We think that belief in God is religion. We consider that to believe is to be religious. If you do not believe, you will be regarded as an atheist and condemned by society. One society condemns those who do not believe in God, and another society condemns those who do. They are both the same.

So religion becomes a matter of belief, and belief acts as a limitation on the mind; and the mind then is never free. But it is only in freedom that you can find out what is true, what is God, not through any belief; because your belief projects what you think God *ought* to be, what you think *ought* to be true. If you believe God is love, God is good, God is this or that, your very belief prevents you from understanding what is God, what is true. But, you see, you want to forget yourself in a belief; you want to sacrifice yourself; you want to emulate another, to abandon this constant struggle that is going on within you and pursue virtue.

Your life is a constant struggle in which there is sorrow, suffering, ambition, transient pleasure, happiness that comes and goes; so the mind wants something enormous to cling to, something beyond itself with which it can become identified. That something the mind calls God, truth, and it identifies itself with it through belief, through conviction, through rationalization, through various forms of discipline and idealistic morality. But that vast something, which creates speculation, is still part of the 'me', it is projected by the mind in its desire to escape from the turmoils of life.

We identify ourselves with a particular country—India, England, Germany, Russia, America. You think of yourself as a Hindu. Why? Why do you identify yourself with India? Have you ever looked at it, gone behind the words that have captured your mind? Living in a city or a small town, leading a miserable life with your struggles and family quarrels, being dissatisfied, discontented, unhappy, you identify yourself with a country called India. This gives you a sense of vastness, of importance, a psychological satisfaction, so you say, "I am an Indian"; and for this you are willing to kill, to die or be maimed.

In the same way, because you are very petty, in constant battle with yourself and others, because you are confused, miserable, uncertain, because you know there is death, you identify yourself with something beyond, something vast, significant, full of meaning, which you call God. This identification with what you call God gives you a sense of enormous importance, and you feel happy. So the identifying of yourself with something vast is a self-expansive process; it is still the struggling of the 'me', the self.

Religion, as we generally know it, is a series of beliefs, dogmas, rituals, superstitions; it is the worship of idols, of charms and gurus, and we think all this will lead us to some ultimate goal. The ultimate goal is our own projection; it is what we want, what we think will make us happy, a guarantee of the deathless state. Caught in this desire for certainty, the mind creates a religion of dogmas, of priestcraft, of superstitions and idol worship; and there it stagnates. Is that religion? Is religion a matter of belief, a matter of accepting or having knowledge of other people's experiences and assertions? Is religion merely the practice of morality? You know, it is comparatively easy to be moral— to do *this* and not to do *that*. You can just imitate a moral system. But behind such morality lurks the aggressive self, growing, expanding, dominating. And is that religion?

You have to find out what truth is, because that is what really matters—not whether you are rich or poor, or whether you are happily married and have children, for all these things come to an end; and there is always death. So, without any form of belief, you must have the vigor, the self-reliance, the initiative to find out for yourself what truth is, what God is. Belief will not free your mind; belief only corrupts, binds, darkens. The mind can be free only through its own vigor and self-reliance.

Surely, it is one of the functions of education to create individuals who are not bound by any form of belief, by any pattern of morality or respectability. It is the 'me' that merely seeks to become moral, respectable. The truly religious individual is he who discovers, who directly experiences what God is, what truth is. That direct experiencing is never possible through any form of belief, through any ritual, through any following or worshipping of another. The truly religious mind is free of all gurus. You as an individual, as you grow and live your life, can discover the truth from moment to moment, and therefore you are capable of being free.

Most people think that to be free from the material things of the world is the first step towards religion. It is not. That is one of the easiest things to do. The first step is to be free to think fully, completely, and independently, which means not being bound by any belief or crushed by circumstances, by environment, so that you are an integrated human being, capable, vigorous, and self-reliant. Only then can your mind, being free, unbiased, unconditioned, find out what God is. Surely, that is the basic purpose for which any educational center should exist: to help each individual who comes there to be free to discover reality. This means not following any system, not clinging to any belief or ritual, and not worshipping any guru. The individual has to awaken his intelligence, not through any form of discipline, resistance, compulsion, coercion, but through freedom. It is only through the intelligence born of freedom that the individual can discover that which is beyond the mind. That immensity—the unnameable, the limitless, that which is not measurable by words and in which there is the love that is not of the mind—must be directly experienced. The mind cannot conceive of it; therefore the mind must be very quiet, astonishingly still, without any demand or any desire. Only then is it possible for that which may be called God or reality to come into being.

Questioner: What is obedience? Should we obey an order even without understanding it?

Krishnamurti: Is that not what most of us do? Parents, teachers, the older people say, "Do this." They say it politely, or with a stick, and because we are afraid, we obey. That is also what governments, what the military people do to us. We are trained from childhood to obey, not knowing what it is all about. The

more authoritarian our parents and the more tyrannical the government, the more we are compelled, shaped from our earliest
years; and without understanding why we should do what we
are told to do, we obey. We are also told what to think. Our
minds are purged of any thought which is not approved by the
state, by the local authorities. We are never taught or helped to
think, to find out, but are required to obey. The priest tells us
what is so, the religious book tells us what is so, and our own
inward fear compels us to obey; because if we do not obey we
shall be confused, we shall feel lost.

So we obey because we are very thoughtless. We don't want
to think because to think is disturbing; to think, we have to
question, to inquire, we have to find out for ourselves. And the
older people don't want us to inquire, they have not the patience
to listen to our questions. They are too busy with their own
quarrels, with their ambitions and prejudices, with their *do's* and
don'ts of morality and respectability; and we who are young are
afraid to go wrong, because we also want to be respectable. Don't
we all want to wear the same kind of clothes, to look alike? We
don't want to do anything different, we don't want to think
independently, to stand apart, because that is very disturbing; so
we join the gang.

Whatever our age, most of us obey, follow, copy, because we
are inwardly frightened of being uncertain. We want to be certain, both financially and morally; we want to be approved of.
We want to be in a safe position, to be enclosed and never to be
confronted with trouble, pain, suffering. It is fear, conscious or
unconscious, that makes us obey the master, the leader, the
priest, the government. It is fear of being punished that prevents
us from doing something harmful to others. So, behind all our
actions, our greeds and pursuits, lurks the desire for certainty,

this desire to be safe, assured. Without being free of fear, merely to obey has little significance. What has significance is to be aware of this fear from day to day, to observe how it shows itself in different ways. Only when there is freedom from fear can there be that inward quality of understanding, that aloneness in which there is no accumulation of knowledge or experience.

.

19

Living Intelligently

When we grow older and leave school after receiving a so-called education, we have to face many problems. What profession are we to choose, so that in it we can fulfill ourselves and be happy? In what vocation or job will we feel that we are not exploiting or being cruel to others? We have to face the problems of suffering, disaster, death. We have to understand starvation, overpopulation, sex, pain, pleasure. We have to deal with the many confusing and contradictory things in life: the wrangles between man and man, between man and woman; the conflicts within and the struggles without. We have to understand ambition, war, the military spirit—and that extraordinary thing called peace, which is much more vital than we realize. We have to comprehend the significance of religion, which is not mere speculation or the worship of images, and also that very strange and complex thing called love. We have to be sensitive to the beauty of life, to a bird in flight—and also to the beggar, to the squalor of the poor, to the hideous buildings that people put up, to the foul road and the still fouler temple. We have to face all these problems. We have to face the question of whom to follow or not to follow, and whether we should follow anyone at all.

Most of us are concerned with bringing about a little change here and there, and with that we are satisfied. The older we grow, the less we want any deep, fundamental change, because we are afraid. We do not think in terms of total transformation, we think only in terms of superficial change; and if you look into it you will find that superficial change is no change at all. It is not a radical revolution, but merely a modified continuity of what has been. All these things you have to face, from your own happiness and misery to the happiness and misery of the many; from your own ambitions and self-seeking pursuits to the ambitions, motivations, and pursuits of others. You have to face competition, the corruption in yourself and in others, the deterioration of the mind, the emptiness of the heart. You have to know all this, you have to face and understand it for yourself. But unfortunately you are not prepared for it.

What have we understood when we leave school? We may have gathered a little knowledge, but we are as dull, empty, shallow as when we came. Our studies, our attending school, our contacts with our teachers have not helped us to understand these very complex problems of life. The teachers are dull, and we become as dull as they are. They are afraid, and we are afraid. So it is our own problem. It is our responsibility as well as the teachers' to see that we go out into the world with maturity, with deep thought, without fear, and are therefore able to face life intelligently.

Now, it appears very important to find an answer to all these complex problems; but there is no answer. All that you can do is to meet these problems intelligently as they arise. Please understand this. Instinctively you want an answer, do you not? You think that by reading books, by following somebody, you will find answers to all the very complex and subtle problems of life. You will find beliefs, theories, but they will not be answers, because these problems have been created by human beings like you. The appalling callousness, the starvation, the cruelty, the hideousness, the squalor—all this has been created by human beings, and to bring about a fundamental transformation you have to understand the human mind and heart, which is your-self. Merely to look for an answer in a book, or to identify yourself with some political or economic system, however much it may promise, or to practice some religious absurdity with its super-stitions, or to follow a guru—none of this will help you to understand these human problems, because they are created by you and others like you. To understand them you must under-stand yourself—understand yourself as you live from moment to moment, from day to day, year in and year out; and for this you need intelligence, a great deal of insight, love, patience.

So you must find out what is intelligence, must you not? You all use that word very freely; but by merely talking about intelli-gence you do not become intelligent. The politicians keep on repeating words like *intelligence, integration, a new culture, a united world,* but they are mere words with very little meaning. So do not use words without really understanding all that they imply.

We are trying to find out what intelligence is—not merely the definition of it, which can be found in any dictionary, but the knowing of it, the feeling of it, the understanding of it; for if we have that intelligence, it will help each one of us, as we grow, to deal with the enormous problems in our life. And without that intelligence, however much we may read, study, accumulate knowledge, reform, bring about little changes here and there in the pattern of society, there can be no real transformation, no lasting happiness.

Now, what does intelligence mean? I am going to find out what it means. Perhaps for some of you this is going to be difficult; but do not bother too much with trying to follow the words; try instead to feel the content of what I am talking about. Try to feel the thing, the quality of intelligence. If you feel it now, then you will, as you grow older, see more and more clearly the significance of what I have been saying.

Most of us think that intelligence is the outcome of acquiring knowledge, information, experience. By having a great deal of knowledge and experience we think we shall be able to meet life with intelligence. But life is an extraordinary thing, it is never stationary; like the river, it is constantly flowing, never still. We think that by gathering more experience, more knowledge, more virtue, more wealth, more possessions, we shall be intelligent. That is why we respect the people who have accumulated knowledge, the scholars, and also the people who are rich and full of experience. But is intelligence the outcome of the 'more'? What is behind this process of having more, wanting more? In wanting more we are concerned with accumulating, are we not?

Now, what happens when you have accumulated knowledge, experience? Whatever further experience you may have is immediately translated in terms of the 'more', and you are never really experiencing, you are always gathering; and this gathering is the process of the mind, which is the center of the 'more'. The 'more' is the 'me', the ego, the self-enclosed entity who is only concerned with accumulating, either negatively or positively. So, with its accumulated experience, the mind meets life. In meeting life with this accumulation of experience, the mind is again seeking the 'more', so it never experiences, it only gathers. As long as the mind is merely an instrument of gathering, there is no real experiencing. How can you be open to experience when you are always thinking of getting something out of that experience, acquiring something more?

So the man who is accumulating, gathering, the man who is desiring more is never freshly experiencing life. It is only when the mind is not concerned with the 'more', with accumulating, that there is a possibility for that mind to be intelligent. When the mind is concerned with the 'more', every further experience strengthens the wall of the self-enclosing 'me', the egocentric process which is the center of all conflict. Please follow this. You think that experience frees the mind, but it does not. As long as your mind is concerned with accumulation, with the 'more', every experience you have only strengthens you in your egotism, in your selfishness, in your self-enclosing process of thought.

Intelligence is possible only when there is real freedom from the self, from the 'me', that is, when the mind is no longer the center of the demand for the 'more', no longer caught up in the desire for greater, wider, more expansive experience. Intelligence is freedom from the pressure of time, is it not? Because the 'more' implies time, and as long as the mind is the center of the demand for the 'more', it is the result of time. So the cultivation of the 'more' is not intelligence. The understanding of this whole process is self-knowledge. When one knows oneself as one is, without an accumulating center, out of that self-knowing comes the intelligence which can meet life; and that intelligence is creative.

Look at your own life. How dull, how stupid, how narrow it is, because you are not creative. When you grow up you may have children, but that is not being creative. You may be a bureaucrat, but in that there is no vitality, is there? It is dead routine, utter boredom. Your life is hedged about by fear, and so there is authority and imitation. You do not know what it is to be creative By creativeness I do not mean painting pictures, writing poems, or being able to sing. I mean the deeper nature of creativeness which, when once discovered, is an eternal source, an undying current; and it can be found only through intelligence. That source is the timeless; but the mind cannot find the timeless as long as it is the center of the 'me', of the self, of the entity that is everlastingly asking for the 'more'.

When you understand all this, not just verbally, but deep down, then you will find that with awakened intelligence there comes a creativeness which is reality, which is God, which is not to be speculated about or meditated upon. You will never get it through your practice of meditation, through your prayers for the 'more' or your escapes from the 'more'. That reality can come into being only when you understand the state of your own mind, the malice, the envy, the complex reactions as they arise from moment to moment every day. In understanding these things there comes a state which may be called love. That love is intelligence, and it brings a creativeness which is timeless.

Questioner: Society is based upon our interdependence. The doctor has to depend on the farmer, and the farmer on the doctor. How then can a man be completely independent?

Krishnamurti: Life is relationship. Even the *sannyasi* has relationship; he may renounce the world, but he is still related to the world. We cannot escape from relationship. For most of us, relationship is a source of conflict; in relationship there is fear, because we psychologically depend on another, either on the husband, on the wife, on the parent, or on a friend. Relationship exists not only between oneself and the parent, between oneself and the child, but also between oneself and the teacher, the cook, the servant, the governor, the commander, and the whole of society; and as long as we do not understand this relationship, there is no freedom from the psychological dependence which brings about fear and exploitation. Freedom comes only through intelligence. Without intelligence, merely to seek independence or freedom from relationship is to pursue an illusion.

So, what is important is to understand our psychological dependence in relationship. It is in uncovering the hidden things of the heart and mind, in understanding our own loneliness, emptiness, that there is freedom, not from relationship, but from the psychological dependence which causes conflict, misery, pain, fear.

Questioner: Why is truth unpalatable?

Krishnamurti: If I think I am very beautiful and you tell me I am not, which may be a fact, do I like it? If I think I am very intelligent, very clever, and you point out that I am actually a rather silly person, it is very unpalatable to me. And your pointing out my stupidity gives you a sense of pleasure, does it not? It flatters your vanity, it shows how clever *you* are. But you do not want to look at your own stupidity; you want to run away from what you are, you want to hide from yourself, you want to cover up your own emptiness, your own loneliness. So you seek out friends who never tell you what you are. You want to show others what they are; but when others show you what you are, you do not like it. You avoid that which exposes your own inner nature.

Questioner: Up to now our teachers have been very certain and have taught us in the usual way, but after listening to what has been said here and after taking part in the discussions, they have become very uncertain. An intelligent student will know how to conduct himself under these circumstances; but what will those do who are not intelligent?

Krishnamurti: What are the teachers uncertain about? Not about what to teach, because they can carry on with mathematics, geography, the usual curriculum. That is not what they are uncertain about. They are uncertain about how to deal with the student, are they not? They are uncertain in their relationship with the student. Until recently they were never particularly concerned about their relationship with the student; they just came to the class, taught, and went out. But now they are concerned as to whether they are creating fear by exercising their authority to make the student obey. They are concerned as to whether they are repressing the student, or are encouraging his initiative and helping him to find his true vocation. Naturally all this has made them uncertain. But surely the teacher as well as the student has to be uncertain; he too has to inquire, to search. That is the whole process of life from the beginning to the end, is it not?—never to stop in a certain place and say, "I know."

An intelligent man is never static, he never says, "I know." He is always inquiring, always uncertain, always looking, searching, finding out. The moment he says, "I know," he is already dead. And whether we are young or old, most of us—because of tradition, compulsion, fear, because of bureaucracy and the absurdities of our religion—are all but dead, without vitality, without vigor, without self-reliance. So the teacher has also to find out. He has to discover for himself his own bureaucratic tendencies and cease to deaden the minds of others; and that is a very difficult process. It requires a great deal of patient understanding.

So the intelligent student has to help the teacher, and the

teacher has to help the student; and both have to help the dull boy or girl who is not very intelligent. That is relationship. Surely, when the teacher himself is uncertain, inquiring, he is more tolerant, more hesitant, more patient and affectionate with the dull student, whose intelligence may thereby be awakened.

Questioner: The farmer has to rely on the doctor for the cure of physical pain. Is this also a dependent relationship?

Krishnamurti: As we have seen, if psychologically I depend on you, my relationship with you is based on fear; and as long as fear exists, there is no independence in relationship. The problem of freeing the mind from fear is quite complex.

You see, what is important is not what one says in answer to all these questions, but for you to find out for yourself the truth of the matter by constant inquiry—which means not being caught in any belief or system of thought. It is constant inquiry that creates initiative and brings about intelligence. Merely to be satisfied with an answer dulls the mind. So it is very important for you not just to accept, but to inquire constantly and begin to discover freely for yourself the whole meaning of life.

20

Being Educated Rightly

I wonder why you are being educated? Do you know? As soon as you are old enough your parents send you to school. They perhaps know why they send you to school, but do you know why you go to school? All that you and your parents know is that you must go to school and be educated.

Now, what does it mean to be educated? Have you ever thought about it? Does it mean merely passing examinations so that afterwards you can get married and have some sort of job which you may or may not like, and continue in that job for the rest of your life? Is that education?

You are in various schools and you are being educated, that is, you are learning mathematics, history, geography, science, and so on. Why? Have you ever wondered? Is it merely in order to earn a living afterwards? Is that the purpose of education? Is education merely a matter of passing examinations and putting a few letters after your name, or is it something entirely different?

If you look around, you will see what an awful mess the world is in. Do you see the poor who have very little to eat, who have no holidays and must work day after day from morning till night, while your parents go to the club in luxurious cars and enjoy themselves there? That is life, is it not? There are the poor and the rich, those who are ill and those who have good health, and throughout the world there are wars, there are miseries, there is every kind of trouble. And should you not begin to think about these things while you are young? But, you see, you are not helped in your schools to prepare yourself to meet that vast expanse of life with its extraordinary struggles, miseries, suffering, wars; nobody talks to you about all this. They just tell you the bare facts, but that is not enough, is it?

Surely, education is not just to enable you to get a job; it is something which should help you to prepare for life. You may become a clerk, or a governor, or a scientist, but that is not the whole of life.

There are all kinds of things in life. Life is like the ocean. The ocean is not just what you see on the surface, is it? It is tremendously deep, it has enormous currents and is teeming with all kinds of life, with many varieties of fish, the big living on the small. All that is the sea; and so it is with life, in which there are all kinds of enjoyments, pleasures, pains, extraordinary inventions, innumerable systems of meditation, and the mass search for happiness. The whole of that is life, but you are not prepared for it. At school nobody talks to you about all those things. There are too many boys and girls in each class, and the teacher is only concerned with helping you to pass the examinations, he is not interested in the clarification of your minds. But education is surely not a process of stuffing the mind with information. If you know how to read you can pick up any encyclopedia and get whatever information you want. So I think education is something entirely different from merely learning certain facts and passing a few examinations.

You see, as long as we are afraid, we are not educated. Do you know what fear is? You know you are afraid. The children are afraid, the grown-up people are afraid, you are all afraid; and as long as we are afraid, we are not educated, we have no intelligence. So education is not merely the stuffing of the mind with information, but the helping of the student to understand without fear this great complexity of life.

You are afraid of your teachers, of your parents, of your elder brother, of your aunt, or of somebody else, are you not? The older people have the power to punish you, to push you away or ask you to stay in your own room; and so in the school as well as in the home we are continually trained in fear. Our life is molded by fear, and from childhood till we die we are afraid. And do you know what fear does? Have you ever watched yourself when you are afraid, how your tummy tightens up, how you perspire, how you get nightmares? You don't like to be with the people of whom you are frightened, do you? You want to run away like an animal that is threatened. You see, with that fear we go to school and college, and with that fear we leave college to meet this extraordinary thing, this vast stream with its enormous depth which we call life. So it seems to me that the thing of first importance in education is to see to it that we are educated to be free from fear; because fear dulls our minds, fear cripples our thinking, fear makes for darkness, and as long as we are frightened we shall not create a new world. Do you understand what I am talking about, or is it something of which you have never heard before?

You know, in the world outside of your own family, outside of your home, in the world beyond Bombay, in Europe, America, and Russia, they are preparing instruments of enormous destruction. The world is going through an awful phase, and all the politicians, all the leaders are very confused, though they say they are not, for they are always having wars, there is always some kind of trouble. So the world at present is not a beautiful thing, it is not a happy place to live in; and if you who are very young are not rightly educated, you will obviously create a world which is equally unhappy, equally miserable, equally confused. Is it not therefore very important to find out how you should be educated so that you can create a totally different kind of world?—a world in which we can all live happily together, in which there are not the rich and the poor, neither the big politicians who have all the power, position, glamour, nor the underprivileged who have nothing in life and must work without ceasing till they die.

It is you who will have to create a new world, not the old people, because the old people are making an awful mess of it. But if you are rightly educated you can create a new world. It is in your hands, not in the hands of the politicians or the priests. If you are rightly educated you will create a marvelous world—not a world of India or Europe, but a world which will be *ours*, yours and mine, a world in which we shall all live happily together. And I assure you, the creation of such a world depends on you, not on anybody else, and that is why it is very important how you are educated and what kind of teachers you have. If the teacher is afraid, he will have students who are also afraid. If the teacher is narrow, petty, small, merely passing on information to you, then you too will have minds which are very small and you will grow up without understanding what life is.

So it is really very important to be educated rightly, which means growing up in freedom; and you cannot be free if you are frightened of your parents, of your teachers, of public opinion, or of what your grandmother would say. If you are frightened you can never be free. And you may notice in the schools that the teachers have not thought out this problem of fear; because the moment you have any kind of compulsion to make you do something, either through so-called kindness or through a system of discipline, it does create fear. If I am the teacher, and in order to make you study I compare you with another student, saying that you are not as intelligent as some other boy or girl, I am destroying you, am I not? In our present schools we have examinations, which breed fear, and we also have systems of grading, which means that the student is always being compared with somebody else; therefore it is the clever boy or girl who is considered important, and not the individual student. The student who is very smart at his studies, who has a peculiar capacity to pass examinations, may be stupid in other directions, and probably he is.

Giving marks, grading, comparing, and any form of compulsion, either through kindness or through threats, breeds fear; and it is because we are caught in this fear while we are young that we struggle in fear for the rest of our life. The older people, by their attitude towards life, create a form of education which is merely a repetition of the old, so there is no new way of living. That is why it seems to me very important to think about all these matters while you are still very young. Even if you don't understand what I am saying you should ask your teachers about this, if they will permit it, and see if you can really be free from fear. When there is no fear, you study much better. When you feel that you are not being compelled to do anything, you will find out what you are interested in, and then for the rest of your life you will do something which you really love to do—which is much more important than becoming a miserable clerk because you must have a job. To do something because your parents say that you must do it, or because society demands it, is all nonsense; whereas, if you really love to do something with your hands and with your mind, then through that love you will create a new world. But you cannot create a new world if you are frightened, and therefore while you are young there must be a spirit of revolt.

Do you understand what revolt is? As you grow from childhood to adulthood, life presses in upon you in the form of parents, teachers, tradition, neighbors, the culture or society in which you are brought up, and so on; all this encloses you like a prison and compels you to do what *it* wants, so you are never yourself. And is it not very important that education should help you to be free so that you can think and live without fear and thereby know for yourself what love is? If your parents really love you they will bring about this kind of education, they will see to it that you are free—free to live and grow without fear, free to be happy. But there are very few such parents in the world, because most parents say that the child must do *this* and not *that*, he must be like his father: a lawyer, a policeman, a merchant, or whatever it is.

It is really very difficult to understand all these complex problems, and as we grow up we can understand them only when there is intelligence. Intelligence should come while we are young, which means that the teacher himself must first understand all this. But there are very few teachers who understand it, because to most of them teaching is merely a job. They cannot get another job where they would make more money, so they say, "Teaching is a good job," which means that they are interested neither in educating you nor in education itself.

So, as a boy or a girl you have to find out the truth of all this, you cannot just be tame, like a domesticated animal. I hope you are understanding what I am talking about, because all this is really very difficult and requires a great deal of thinking on your part. The world is disintegrating, going to pieces, there are wars, starvation, and misery; and the creation of a new world is in your hands. But you cannot create a new world if in you there is no spirit of revolt; and you cannot have this spirit of revolt as long as there is fear which cripples intelligence.

Questioner: I have everything to make me happy, while others have not. Why is this so?

Krishnamurti: Why do you think it is like that? You may have good health, kind parents, a good brain, and therefore think you are happy; whereas, somebody who is ill, whose parents are unkind, and who has not too good a brain, feels that he is unhappy. Now, why is this so? Why are you happy while somebody else is unhappy? Does happiness consist in having riches, cars, good houses, clean food, kind parents? Is that what you call happiness? And is a person unhappy who has none of these things? So, what do you mean by happiness? This is important to find out, is it not? Does happiness consist in comparing? When you say, "I am happy," is your happiness born of comparison? Do you understand what I am talking about, or is this too difficult?

Have you not heard your parents say, "So-and-so is not as well off as we are"? Comparison makes us feel that we have something, it gives us a sense of satisfaction, does it not? If one is clever and compares oneself with somebody who is not so clever, one feels very happy. That is, we think we are happy through pride, comparison; but the man who feels happy by comparing himself with another who has a little less is a most miserable human being, because there is always somebody above him who has more; and so it goes on and on. Surely, comparison is not happiness. Happiness is entirely different; it is not a thing to be sought after. Happiness comes when you are doing something because you really love to do it, and not because it gives you riches or makes you a prominent person.

Questioner: What is the way to get rid of the fear that we have?

Krishnamurti: First you must know what you are afraid of, must you not? You may be afraid of your parents, of the teachers, of not passing an examination, of what your sister, your brother, or your neighbor might say; or you may be afraid of not being as good or as clever as your father, who has a big name. There are many kinds of fear, and one must know what one is afraid of.

Now, do you know what you are afraid of? If you do, then don't run away from that fear, but find out why you are afraid. If you want to know how to get rid of fear, you must not escape from it, you must face it; and the very facing of it helps you to be free of it. As long as we are running away from fear, we do not look at it; but the moment we stop and look at fear, it begins to dissolve. The very running away is the cause of fear.

You must be teeming with questions, but perhaps you are shy. May I ask you a question? What do you want to be when you grow up? Do you know? Of course, for the girls it is simple, they want to get married, that is understood; but even if you get married, what do you want to do? Are you ambitious? Do you know what ambition is? It is the desire to become somebody, is it not? The man who has an ideal and says, "I am going to be like Rama, Sita, or Gandhiji," is still ambitious. Are you ambitious in some way?

Now, what does that mean? Why are you ambitious? This may be a little difficult, but it is one of the problems of life and you ought to be thinking about it. I will tell you why. We are all ambitious; everyone is ambitious in his own way. And do you know what that does? It causes us to be against one another. We are always struggling to be rich, to have fame, to be more clever; I want to be greater than you, and you want to be greater than I. So ambition really means trying to be something we are not. And which is important? To try to be something we are not, or to understand what we are? Surely, we must first look at ourselves and begin to understand what we are.

You see, most of us are idealists; and idealists are hypocrites, because they are always trying to become something which they are not. If I am stupid and I strive to become clever, everybody thinks it is a marvelous thing. But a stupid person, however well he may learn the tricks of cleverness, does not thereby become intelligent. Whereas, if I know that I am stupid, then that very knowledge is the beginning of intelligence—which is much better than merely being clever. Do you understand?

If I am not very quick witted, what generally happens? In school I am put at the end of the class—which is a disgraceful thing for the teacher to do, because I am as important as anybody else. It is stupid of the teacher to keep me at the end of the class by comparing me with the clever students, because by comparing he is destroying me.

But comparison is the basis of our so-called education, and of our whole culture. The teacher is always saying that you must do as well as such and such a boy or girl, so you struggle to be as clever as they are. And what happens to you? You get more and more worried, physically ill, mentally worn out. Whereas, if the teacher does not compare you with anyone, but says, "Look here, old boy, be yourself. Let us find out what you are interested in, what your capacities are. Don't imitate, don't try to become like Rama, Sita, or Gandhiji, but be what you are and begin from there"—if the teacher says that, then it is *you* who are important, not somebody else. It is the individual who is important, and by comparing a student with somebody who is cleverer, the teacher is belittling him, making him smaller, more stupid. It is the function of the teacher to help you to find out what you are, and he cannot help you to do that if he is comparing you with somebody else. Comparison destroys you, so don't compare yourself with another. You are as good as anybody. Understand what you are, and from there begin to find out how to be more fully, more freely, more expansively what you are.

Questioner: You said that if the parents really love their child they will not stop him from doing anything. But if the child does not want to be clean or eats something which is bad for his health, must we not stop him?

Krishnamurti: I do not think I have ever said that if the parents love their child they will let him do exactly as he likes. Sir, this is a very difficult question, is it not? After all, if I love my son I shall see to it that he has no cause for fear—which is an extraordinarily difficult thing to do. As I said, to be free of fear, the child must not be compared with anyone else, nor must he be subjected to examinations. If I love the child I shall give him freedom, not to do what he likes—because merely to do what one likes is stupid—but freedom in which to cultivate intelligence; and that intelligence will then tell him what to do.

To have intelligence there must be freedom, and you cannot be free if you are constantly being urged to become like some hero, for then the hero is important and not you. Don't you have tummy-aches when you have examinations? Don't you feel nervous, anxious? When year after year you have to face this terrible ordeal called examinations, do you know what it does to you throughout the rest of your life? The older people say that you must grow without fear; but it doesn't mean a thing, it is only a lot of words, because they are cultivating fear through subjecting you to examinations and by comparing you with somebody else.

Another thing we should really discuss is what we call discipline. Do you know what I mean by discipline? From childhood you are told what to do, and you have jolly well got to do it. No one takes the trouble to explain why you should get up early, why you should be clean. Parents and teachers do not explain these things to you because they have neither the love, the time, nor the patience; they merely say, "Do it or I shall punish you." So education, as we know it, is the instilling of fear. And how can your mind be intelligent when there is fear? How can you have love or feel respect for people when you are afraid? You may "respect" the people who have big names, expensive cars; but you don't respect your servant, you just kick him. When a big man comes around you all salute him and touch his feet, and that is called respect; but it is not respect, it is fear that is making you touch his feet. You don't touch the feet of the poor *coolie*, do you? You are not respectful to him, because he cannot give you anything. So all our education is nothing but the cultivation or strengthening of fear. That is a terrible thing, is it not? And as long as there is fear, how can we create a new world? We cannot. That is why it is very important to understand this problem of fear while you are young, and for all of us to see to it that we are really educated without fear.

Questioner: Is it not important to have ideals in life?

Krishnamurti: This is a good question, because you all have ideals. You have the ideal of nonviolence, the ideal of peace, or the ideal of a person such as Rama, Sita, or Gandhiji, have you not? Which means what? You are not important, but the ideal is very important. Rama is awfully important, but not poor old you, so you imitate him. All that you are concerned with is to copy either a person or an idea. As I said, an idealist is a hypocrite, because he is always trying to become what he is not, instead of being and understanding what he is.

You see, the problem of idealism is really a complex one, and you don't understand it because you have never been encouraged to think about it; no one has ever talked it over with you. All your books, all your teachers, all the newspapers and magazines say you must have ideals, you must be like this hero or that, which only makes the mind like a monkey who imitates, or like a gramophone record which repeats a lot of words. So you must not accept, but begin to question everything and find out; and you cannot question if you are inwardly afraid. To question everything means being in revolt, which is to create a new world. But you see, your teachers and parents do not want you to be in revolt, because they want to control you, they want to shape and mold you into their patterns; and so life continues to be an ugly thing.

Questioner: If we are small, how can we create a new world?

Krishnamurti: You cannot create a new world if you are small. But you are not going to be small for the rest of your life, are you? You are small if you are afraid. You may have a big body, a big car, a high position, but if you are afraid inside you will never create a new world. That is why it is very important to grow with intelligence, without fear, to grow in freedom. But to grow in freedom does not mean disciplining oneself to be free.

Questioner: What should be the system of education to make the child fearless?

Krishnamurti: A system or a method implies being told what to do and how to do it; and will that make you fearless? Can you be educated with intelligence, without fear, through any kind of system? When you are young, you should be free to grow; but there is no system to make you free. A system implies making the mind conform to a pattern, does it not? It means locking you up in a framework, not giving you freedom. The moment you rely on a system you dare not step out of it, and then the very thought of stepping out of it breeds fear. So there is really no *system* of education. What is important is the teacher and the student, not the system. After all, if I want to help you to be free of fear, I myself must be free of fear. Then I must study you; I must take the trouble to explain everything to you and tell you what the world is like; and to do all this I must love you. As a teacher I must have the feeling that when you leave school or college you should be without fear. If I really have that feeling, I can help you to be free of fear.

Questioner: Is it possible to know the quality of gold without testing it in a special way? Similarly, can the capacity of each child be known without some sort of examination?

Krishnamurti: Do you really know the capacity of the child through examination? One child may fail because he is nervous, fearful of the examination, while another may slip through because he is less affected by it. Whereas, if you watch each child week after week, if you observe his character, the way he plays games, the way he talks, the interests he shows, how he studies, the food he eats, then you will begin to know the child without requiring examinations to tell you what he is capable of. But we have never thought about all these things.

Questioner: Sir, what is your idea of a new world?

Krishnamurti: I have no idea about the new world. The "new world" cannot be new if I have an idea about it. This is not just a clever statement, it is a fact. If I have an idea about it, the idea is born of my study and experience, is it not? It is born of what I have learnt, of what I have read, of what other people have said the new world should be. So the "new world" can never be new if it is a creation of the mind, because the mind is the old. You don't know what is going to happen tomorrow, do you? You may know that there will be no school tomorrow because it is Sunday, and that on Monday you will be going to school again; but what is going to happen outside the school, what kind of feelings you are going to have, what kind of things you are going to see—all that you don't know, do you? Because you don't know what is going to happen tomorrow, or the next morning, when it happens it will be new; and to be able to meet the new is what matters.

Questioner: How can we create anything new if we don't know what it is we want to create?

Krishnamurti: It is a sad thing not to know what it means to create, is it not? When you have a feeling, you may put what you feel into words. If you see a beautiful tree, you may write a poem describing not the tree, but what the tree has awakened in you.

That feeling is the new, it is the creative thing; but you cannot bring it about, it must happen to you.

Questioner: Must the children take all these matters seriously? And if they do, will they ever be free to enjoy themselves?

Krishnamurti: Are you not serious now? But you cannot be serious all the time, can you? You cannot play all the time, or sleep all the time, or study all the time. There is a time to play and a time to be serious, and this meeting is meant to be serious; but if you do not want to be serious, it is all right, nobody is going to compel you.

21

Religion Really Is a Process of Education

We have been talking about fear; and do you not think that what we *call* religion is really the outcome of fear? You must have noticed how your parents, your grandparents, or your relatives go to the temple, worship an idol, repeat sentences from the Gita or some other sacred book, or perform some ritual. Doing these things and believing in something is what they call religion. But do you think it is so? Going to the temple, putting flowers at the foot of an idol made by the hand, doing some ritual day after day, year in and year out till you die—is that religion?

And if religion is not the worship of a thing made by the hand, then is it the worship of something made by the mind? When you enter a temple you see there an idol which some sculptor has carved out of stone. People put flowers before this image, they pour water on it, they clothe it; that is what they call religion, and they think it is irreligious not to do these things.

We also have an idea of what God is, and that idea is created by the mind, is it not? The idol is made by the mind through the hand, and the idea of God is made and held in the mind as something marvelous, something to be worshipped like the sacred idol. Both the idea and the idol are made by the mind, are they not? Obviously they are not God, because the mind has invented them. In Europe you will see the sculptured figure of a human being stripped and nailed on a cross, and that figure they worship. Here in India we do the same thing in a different way. Whether in India, in Europe or America, we pray to an image, we worship an idea, and gradually we build up a thing called religion—a religion which is invented by the mind.

You see, we are afraid to be alone, we want somebody to help us. At your age we want to be helped by our mother, by our father, by our grandfather, and as we grow older we still want somebody to help us, because life is very difficult; we want a glorified father to protect us, to tell us what to do. So, out of the fear of being lonely, of not being helped, we believe in a God who is going to help us; but it is still an invention of the mind, is it not? Because we are afraid and want to be guided and told what is right and what is wrong, as we grow up we create a religion which is not religion at all. Religion, I think, is something totally different, and to find the real thing we must obviously be free of the thing which man invents. Do you follow? To find out what God is, to discover something that is real, one must be free of all the pseudoreligious trappings that man has imposed upon himself. You can discover the real thing only if you are completely free of fear, which means that as you grow up and go out into the world you must have the intelligence to find out what you are afraid of—to take it out of the cupboard of your mind, look at it and not run away from it.

Most of us are afraid to be alone. Do we ever go out for a walk alone? Very rarely. We always want somebody to go with us because we want to chatter, we want to tell somebody a story, we are all the time talking, talking, talking; so we are never alone, are we? When one grows older and can go for a walk alone, one discovers a great many things. One discovers one's own ways of thinking, and then one begins to observe all the things about one—the beggar, the stupid man, the clever man, the rich and the poor; one becomes aware of the trees, the birds, the light on a leaf. You will see all this when you go out alone. In being alone you will soon find out that you are afraid. And it is because we are afraid that we have invented this thing called religion.

Volumes have been written about God and what you should do to approach him; but the basis of it all is fear. As long as one is afraid, one cannot find anything real. If you are afraid of the dark, you dare not go out, so you pull up the sheet and go to sleep. To go out and look, to find out what is real, there must be freedom from fear, must there not? But you see, to be free from fear is very difficult. Most grown-up people say that you can be free only when you are older, when you have gathered knowledge and have learned to discipline your mind. They think freedom is something very far away, at the end, not at the beginning. But, surely, there must be freedom right from child-hood up, otherwise you are never free.

You see, being themselves frightened, the older people discipline you, they tell you what is right and what is wrong; they say you must do *that* and not *this*, that you must think of what people will say, and so on. There is every form of control to make you fit into the groove, into a frame, a pattern, and this is called discipline. Being very young, and out of your own fear, you fit in; but that does not help you, because when you just fit in you do not understand.

Now, look at it the other way. If you were not disciplined, if you were not controlled, held down, would you do what you like? Would you do as you please if there were nobody to tell you what you should do? You probably would now, because you are used to being forced, held down, put in a framework, and as a reaction you would do something contrary to it. But suppose that from childhood up, right from the beginning as you go through school, the teacher talked things over with you and did not tell you what you *should* do—how then would you respond? If, right from the beginning as you go through school, the teacher pointed out that to be free is the first thing, not the last thing when you are about to die, then what would happen?

The difficulty is that to be free demands a great deal of intelligence; and as you don't yet know what it is to be free—free to do something which you really love to do—it is the function of the teacher to help you to discover the ways of intelligence. It is intelligence which brings about freedom from fear. As long as there is fear, you are constantly imposing upon yourself a kind of discipline: I must do *this* and not *that*, I must believe, I must conform, I must do *puja*, and so on. This self-discipline is all born of fear, and where there is fear there is no intelligence.

So education, rightly speaking, is not just a matter of reading books, passing examinations, and getting a job. Education is quite a different process; it extends from the moment you are born to the moment you die. You may read innumerable books and be very clever, but I do not think mere cleverness is a mark of education. If you are merely clever you miss a great deal in life. The important thing is first to find out what you are afraid of, to understand it and not run away from it. When your mind is really free from demands of every kind, when it is no longer envious, acquisitive, only then can you find out what God is. God is not what people say God is. God is something entirely different—something that comes into being when you understand, when you have no fear.

So, religion is really a process of education, is it not? Religion is not a matter of what to believe and what not to believe, of doing rituals or clinging to some superstitions; it is a process of educating ourselves in the ways of understanding so that our life becomes extraordinarily rich and we are no longer frightened, mediocre human beings. Only then can we create a new world.

Politicians and religious leaders say that the creation of a new world is in the hands of the young people. Haven't you heard that? Hundreds of times, probably. But they don't educate you to be free; and there must be freedom to create a new world. The grown-ups educate you in the pattern of their own ideas—and they have made an awful mess of things. They say it is you, the younger generation, who must create a new world; but at the same time they put you into a cage, do they not? They tell you that you must be an Indian, a Parsi, this or that—and if you follow their ideas, you are obviously going to create a world exactly like the present one. A new world can be created only when you create out of freedom, not out of fear, not out of superstition, nor on the basis of what certain people have said the new world should be.

You who are young, the coming generation, can bring about a totally different world only if you are educated to be free, and are not forced to do something which you do not love or understand. That is why it is very important, while you are young, to be *real* revolutionaries—which means not accepting anything, but inquiring into all these things to find out what is true. Only then can you create a new world. Otherwise, though you may call it by a different name, you will perpetuate the same old world of misery and destruction which has always existed until now.

But generally what happens to us when we are young? The girls get married, have children, and gradually wither away. The boys, when they grow up, have to earn a livelihood, so they get jobs and are required to conform, forced to follow a profession whether they like it or not; being married and having children, they are dragged along by their responsibilities and must there-fore do what they are told. So the spirit of revolt, the spirit of inquiry, the spirit of inward search comes to an end; all their rev-olutionary ideas of creating a new world are crushed out, be-cause life is too much for them. They have to go to the office, they have a boss there for whom they must do this or that, and gradu-ally the sense of inquiry, the feeling of revolt, the eagerness to create an altogether different way of life is completely destroyed. That is why it is very important to have this spirit of revolt right from the beginning, from childhood up.

You see, religion, the real thing, means a revolt in order to find God, which is to discover for oneself what is true. It is not a mere acceptance of the so-called sacred books, however ancient and venerated they may be.

Questioner: In your book on education you suggest that modern education is a complete failure. I would like you to explain this.

Krishnamurti: Is it not a failure, sir? When you go out on the street you see the poor man and the rich man; and when you look around you, you see all the so-called educated people throughout the world wrangling, fighting, killing each other in wars. There is now scientific knowledge enough to enable us to provide food, clothing, and shelter for all human beings, yet it is not done. The politicians and other leaders throughout the world are educated people, they have titles, degrees, caps and gowns, they are doctors and scientists; and yet they have not created a world in which man can live happily. So modern edu-cation has failed, has it not? And if you are satisfied to be educated in the same old way, you will make another howling mess of life.

Questioner: May I know why we should not fit into our parents' plans, since they want us to be good?

Krishnamurti: Why should you fit into your parents' plans, however worthy, however noble they may be? You are not just putty, you are not jelly to be fitted into a mold. And if you do fit in, what happens to you? You become a so-called good girl, or good boy, and then what? Do you know what it means to be good? Goodness is not just doing what society says, or what your parents say. Goodness is something entirely different, is it not? Goodness comes into being only when you have intelligence, when you have love, when you have no fear. You cannot be good if you are afraid. You can become respectable by doing what society demands— and then society gives you a garland, it says what a good person you are; but merely being respectable is not being good.

You see, when we are young we do not want to fit in, and at the same time we want to be good. We want to be nice, to be sweet, we want to be considerate and do kind things; but we do not know what it all means, and we are "good" because we are afraid. Our parents say, "Be good," and most of us are good, but such "goodness" is merely living according to their plans for us.

Questioner: You say that modern education is a failure. But if the politicians had not been educated, do you think they could have created a better world?

Krishnamurti: I am not at all sure that they couldn't have created a better world if they had never received this kind of education. What does it mean to govern the people? After all, that is what politicians are supposed to do—to govern the people. But they are ambitious, they want power, position, they want to be respected, they want to be the leaders, to have the first place; they are not thinking of the people, they are thinking of themselves or their parties, which are an extension of themselves. Human beings are human beings, whether they live in India, in Germany, in Russia, in America, or in China; but you see, by dividing human beings according to countries, more politicians can have big jobs, so they are not interested in thinking of the world as a whole. They are "educated," they know how to read, how to argue, and they talk everlastingly about being good citizens—but they must have the first place. To divide up the world and create wars—is that what we call education? The politicians are not alone in doing this; we all do it. Some people want war because it gives them profit. So it is not only the politicians who must have the right kind of education.

Questioner: Then what is your idea of the right kind of education?

Krishnamurti: I have just told you. Look, I will show you again. After all, the religious person is not one who worships a god, an image made by the hand or by the mind, but one who is really inquiring into what truth is, what God is; and such a person is really educated. He may not go to a school, he may have no books, he may not even know how to read; but he is freeing himself from fear, from his egotism, from his selfishness, ambition. So education is not merely a process of learning how to read, how to calculate, how to build bridges, how to do scientific research in order to find new ways of utilizing atomic power, and all the rest of it. The function of education is primarily to help man to free himself from his own pettiness and from his stupid ambitions. All ambition is stupid, petty—there is no great ambition. And education also implies helping the student to grow in freedom without fear, does it not?

Questioner: How can every man be educated like that?

Krishnamurti: Don't you want to be educated like that?

Questioner: But how?

Krishnamurti: First, do you want to be educated like that? Don't ask how, but have the feeling that you want to be educated in that way. If you have this intense feeling, as you grow up you will help to create it in others, will you not? Sir, look: if you are very keen on playing a certain game, you soon find other people to play it with you. Similarly, if you are really keen to be educated in the way we have been discussing, then you will help to create a school with the right kind of teachers who will provide that kind of education. But most of us don't really want that kind of education, and so we ask, "How can it be brought about?" We look to somebody else for the answer. But if all of you—every student who is listening, and I hope the teachers too—want that kind of education, then you will demand it and bring it into being.

Take a simple example. You know what chewing gum is, don't you? If you all want chewing gum, the manufacturer produces it, but if you don't want it the manufacturer goes broke. Similarly on quite a different level, if you all say, "We want the right kind of education, not this phony education which only leads to organized murder"—if you say that and really mean it, you will bring into being the right kind of education. But you see, you are still too young, too frightened, and that is why it is important to help you to create this thing.

Questioner: If I want the right kind of education, do I need teachers?

Krishnamurti: Of course you do. You need teachers to help you, do you not? But what is help? You are not living in the world alone, are you? There are your fellow students, your parents, your teachers, the postman, the man who brings the milk—everybody is needed, we all help each other to live in this world. But if you say, "The teacher is sacred, he is at one level and I am at another," then that kind of help is no help at all. The teacher is helpful only if he is not using teaching to feed his vanity or as a means of his own security. If he is teaching, not because he is unable to do anything else, but because he really loves to teach, then he will help the student to grow without fear. This means no examinations, no grading, no marks. If you are to create the right kind of education, you need such teachers to help you to create it; so it is very important for the teachers themselves to be rightly educated.

Questioner: If all ambitions are stupid, then how can man progress?

Krishnamurti: Do you know what progress is? Now, have patience and let us go into it slowly. What is progress? Have you ever thought about it? Is it progress when you can get to Europe in a few hours by airplane instead of taking a fortnight to get there by boat? The invention of faster means of transportation and communication, the development of bigger guns, bigger and better ways of destroying each other, wiping out thousands of people with a single atomic bomb instead of shooting them down one by one with arrows—this we call progress, do we not? So there has been progress in the technological sense; but have we progressed in any other direction? Have we stopped wars? Are people more kind, more loving, more generous, more thoughtful, less cruel? You don't have to say yes or no, but just look at the facts.

Scientifically and physically we have made tremendous progress; but inwardly we are at a standstill, are we not? For most of us education has been like lengthening only one leg of a tripod so we have no balance; and yet we talk about progress, all the newspapers are full of it!

Questioner: I have a friend who hates her parents because they have separated her from a person she loves. How can I help her?

Krishnamurti: This is a very complicated question, is it not? You know, life is not very easy, some parts of it are very cruel. There are thoughtless parents who are not concerned with their children at all; or if they are concerned, they want the children to obey, to imitate, to do everything exactly as the parents wish. So resistance is gradually built up in the children, is it not? If the father happens to be intelligent, and the mother stupidly insistent when the father is not there, or vice versa, the children have resistance, antagonism to one parent or the other. Perhaps you can help your friend by being more understanding, more affectionate, and explaining in a kindly manner some of the things which you and I have talked about and which you understand for yourself.

You see, the moment you have a grudge, the moment you hate somebody, it harms you far more than the person you dislike, because that feeling is like a wound inside you that is festering, but it is very difficult for children, for young people to understand all this. After all, children are full of mischief, full of happy play—as they should be; and if parents force their child into a particular pattern or mold, it creates in the child a tremendous resistance, a blind antagonism which he is going to take out on somebody as he grows up. If you have begun to understand this, you can talk it over with your friend and perhaps help her not to build up this hatred, this antagonism within herself.

Questioner: What is the definition of a student?

Krishnamurti: It is very easy to find a definition, is it not? All you have to do is to open a dictionary at the right place and it will give you the answer. But that is not the kind of definition you want, is it? You want to talk about it, you want to find out what a true student is. Is he a true student who passes examinations, gets a job, and then closes all books? Being a student implies studying life, not just reading the few books required by your curriculum; it implies the capacity to observe everything throughout life, not just a few things at a particular period. A student, surely, is not only one who reads, but one who is capable of observing all the movements of life, outward and inward, without saying, "This is right, that is wrong." If you condemn something, you don't observe it, do you? To observe you have to study without condemning, without comparing. If I compare you with somebody else, I am not studying you, am I? If I compare you with your younger brother or your elder sister, it is the sister or the brother who is important; therefore I am not studying you.

But our whole education is to compare. You are everlastingly comparing yourself or another with somebody—with your guru, with your ideal, with your father who is so clever, a great politician, and so on. This process of comparison and condemnation prevents you from observing, studying. So a real student is one who observes everything in life, outwardly as well as inwardly, without comparing, approving, or condemning. He is not only capable of research into scientific matters, but is also able to observe the workings of his own mind, his own feelings—which is much more difficult than observing a scientific fact. To understand the whole operation of one's own mind requires a great deal of insight, a great deal of inquiry without condemnation.

Questioner: You say that all idealists are hypocrites. Whom do you call an idealist?

Krishnamurti: Don't you know what an idealist is? If I am violent, I may say that my ideal is to be nonviolent; but the fact remains that I am violent. The ideal is what I hope to be eventually. It will take years for me to become nonviolent, and meanwhile I am violent—that is the real thing. Being violent, I am trying all the time to be nonviolent, which is unreal; and is that not hypocrisy? Instead of understanding and dissolving my violence, I am trying to be something else. The man who is trying to be something other than he is, is obviously a hypocrite. It is like my putting on a mask and saying I am different, but behind the mask I am just the same old man. Whereas, if I can go into the whole process of violence and understand it, then there is a possibility of being free from violence.

22

To Discover the Truth of Things

When you are young you are curious to know all about everything, why the sun shines, what the stars are, all about the moon and the world around us; but as we grow older, knowledge becomes a mere collection of information without any feeling. We become specialists, we know much about this or that subject, and we take very little interest in the things around us, the beggar in the street, the rich man passing by in his car. If we want to know why there are riches and poverty in the world, we can find an explanation. There is an explanation for everything, and explanation seems to satisfy most of us. The same holds true of religion. We are satisfied with explanations; and explaining everything away we call knowledge. And is this what we mean by education? Are we learning to find out, or are we merely asking for explanations, definitions, conclusions, in order to put our minds at rest so that we need not inquire further?

Our elders may have explained everything to us, but our interest has generally been deadened thereby. As we grow older life becomes more complex and very difficult. There are so many things to know, there is so much misery and suffering; and seeing all this complexity, we think we have resolved it all by explaining it away. Someone dies, and it is explained away; so suffering is deadened through explanation. Perhaps we revolt against the idea of war when we are young, but as we grow older we accept the explanation of war, and our minds become dull.

When we are young what is important is not to be satisfied with explanations, but to find out how to be intelligent and thereby discover the truth of things; and we cannot be intelligent if we are not free. It is said that freedom comes only when we are old and wise, but surely there must be freedom while we are still very young—not freedom to do what we like, but freedom to understand very deeply our own instincts and urges. There must be a freedom in which there is no fear, but one cannot be free from fear through an explanation. We are aware of death and the fear of death. By explaining death, can we know what dying is, or be free from the fear of death?

As we grow older it is important to have the capacity to think very simply. What is simplicity? Who is a simple person? A man who lives a hermit's life, who has very few belongings—is he really simple? Is not simplicity something entirely different? Simplicity is of the mind and heart. Most of us are very complex, we have many wants and desires. For example, you want to pass your examinations, you want to get a good job, you have ideals and want to develop a good character, and so on. The mind has so many demands; and does that make for simplicity? Is it not very important to find out?

A complex mind cannot find out the truth of anything, it cannot find out what is real—and that is our difficulty. From childhood we are trained to conform, and we do not know how to reduce complexity to simplicity. It is only the very simple and direct mind that can find the real, the true. We know more and more, but our minds are never simple; and it is only the simple mind that is creative.

When you paint a picture of a tree, what is it you are painting? Are you just painting a picture of the tree as it looks, with its leaves, its branches, its trunk, complete in every detail, or are you painting from the feeling which the tree has awakened in you? If the tree tells you something and you paint from that inner experience, though your feeling may be very complex, the picture that you paint will be the outcome of a great simplicity. It is necessary when you are young to keep your mind very simple, uncontaminated, although you may have all the information you want.

Questioner: If all of us were educated rightly, would we be free of fear?

Krishnamurti: It is very important to be free of fear, is it not? And you cannot be free of fear except through intelligence. So let us first find out how to be intelligent, not how to get rid of fear. If we can experience what it is to be intelligent, then we shall know how to get rid of fear. Fear is always with regard to something, it does not exist by itself. There is the fear of death, the fear of illness, the fear of loss, the fear of one's parents, the fear of what people will say, and so on; and the question is not how to get rid of fear, but how to awaken the intelligence with which to face and to understand and go beyond fear.

Now, how can education help us to be intelligent? What is intelligence? Is it a matter of passing examinations, or being clever? You may read many books, meet prominent people, have a lot of capacity, but does all that make you intelligent? Or, is intelligence something which comes into being only as you become integrated? We are made up of many parts; sometimes we are resentful, jealous, violent, at other times we are humble, thoughtful, calm. At different moments we are different beings; we are never whole, never totally integrated, are we? When a human being has many wants, he is inwardly broken up into many beings.

One must approach the problem simply. The question is how to be intelligent so that you can be rid of fear. If from your earliest childhood whatever difficulty you may have had has been talked over with you so that your understanding of it is not just verbal, but enables you to see the whole of life, then such education can awaken intelligence and thereby free the mind of fear.

Questioner: You have said that to be ambitious is to be stupid and cruel. Is it then stupid and cruel to have the ambition to get the right kind of education?

Krishnamurti: Are you ambitious? What is ambition? When you want to be better than another, to get higher marks than someone else—surely, that is what we call ambition. A little politician is ambitious in wanting to become a big politician; but is it ambitious to want to have the right kind of education? Is it ambition when you do something because you love to do it? When you write or paint—not because you want prestige, but because you love to write or paint—that is not ambition, surely. Ambition comes in when you compare yourself with other writers or artists, when you want to get ahead.

So, it is not ambition when you do something because you really love to do it.

Questioner: When one wants to find truth or peace, one becomes a *sannyasi*. So a *sannyasi* has simplicity?

Krishnamurti: Does one know simplicity when one wants peace? Is it by becoming a *sannyasi* or a *sadhu* that one is simple? Surely, peace is something which is not of the mind. If I want peace, and I try to remove from my mind all thoughts of violence, will that bring me peace? Of if I have many desires and I say that I must have no desire, will I be peaceful? The moment you want something you are in conflict, struggle, and what brings about simplicity is your own understanding of the whole process of wanting.

Questioner: If we are educated in the right way we are free of fear, and if we are educated wrongly we are fearful. Is that true?

Krishnamurti: It is obviously true, is it not? And are we not all afraid of something or other? Everyone is frightened of something—of public opinion, death, disease. That is an obvious fact.

Questioner: If, as you say, everyone is afraid, then no one is a saint or a hero. Are there no great men then in this world?

Krishnamurti: That is mere logical reasoning, is it not? Why should we bother about great men, saints, heroes? What matters is what you are. If you are afraid, you are going to create an ugly world. That is the question, not whether there are great men.

Questioner: You said explanation is a bad thing. We have come here for explanation. Is that bad?

Krishnamurti: I did not say explanation is bad; I said don't be satisfied with explanations.

Questioner: What is your idea about the future of India?

Krishnamurti: I have no idea, no idea at all. I don't think India as India matters very much. What matters is the world. Whether we live in China or Japan, in England, India, or America, we all say, "My country matters very much," and nobody thinks of the world as a whole; history books are full of the constant repetition of wars. If we can begin to understand ourselves as human beings, then perhaps we shall stop killing each other and put an end to wars; but as long as we are nationalistic and think only of our own country, we shall go on creating a terrible world. If once we see that this is *our* earth where we can *all* live happily and at peace, then together we shall build anew; but if we go on thinking of ourselves as Indians, Germans, or Russians, and regard everybody else as foreigners, then there will be no peace and no new world can be created.

Questioner: You say there are very few people in this world who are great. Then what are you?

Krishnamurti: It does not matter what I am. What matters is to find out the truth or the falseness of what is being said. If you think such-and-such a thing is important because so-and-so is saying it, then you are not really listening, you are not trying to find out for yourself what is true and what is false.

But, you see, most of us are afraid to find out for ourselves what is true and what is false, and that is why we merely accept what somebody else says. The important thing is to question, to observe, never to accept. Unfortunately, most of us only listen to those whom we regard as great people, to an established authority, to the Upanishads, the Gita, or whatever it is. We never listen to the birds, to the sound of the sea, or to the beggar. So we miss what the beggar is saying—and there may be truth in what the beggar is saying, and none at all in what is said by the rich man or the man in authority.

Questioner: We read books out of inquisitiveness. When you were young were you not inquisitive?

Krishnamurti: Do you think that merely by reading books you find out for yourself what is true? Do you discover anything by repeating what others have said? Or do you discover only by searching, doubting, never accepting? Many of us read lots of books about philosophy, and this reading shapes our minds— which makes it very difficult to find out for ourselves what is true and what is false. When the mind is already molded, shaped, it can discover the truth only with the greatest difficulty.

Questioner: Should we not be concerned about the future?

Krishnamurti: What do you mean by the future? Twenty or fifty years hence—is that what you mean by the future? The future that is many years away is very uncertain, is it not? You do not know what is going to happen, so what is the good of being troubled or disturbed about it? There may be a war, an epidemic; anything may happen, so the future is uncertain, it is unknown. What matters is how you are living now, what you are thinking, feeling now. The present, which is today, matters very much, not tomorrow or what is going to happen twenty years hence; and to understand the present requires a great deal of intelligence.

Questioner: When we are young we are very playful and do not always know what is good for us. If a father advises his son for the good of the son, should not the son follow his father's advice?

Krishnamurti: What do *you* think? If I am a parent, I must first find out what my son really wants to do in life, must I not? Does the parent know enough about the child to advise him? Has the parent studied the child? How can a parent who has very little time to observe his child offer him advice? It sounds nice to say that the father should guide his son; but if the father does not know his son, then what is to be done? A child has his own propensities and capacities which have to be studied, not just for a certain time or at a particular place, but throughout the period of his childhood.

Questioner: You said last time that the idealist is a hypocrite. If we want to construct a building, we must first have an idea of it. Similarly, must we not first have an ideal if we are to bring about a new world?

Krishnamurti: To have an idea of a building which you want to construct is not the same as being idealistic about something. Surely, they are two different things.

Questioner: By aiming at the well-being of our own country, do we not also aim at the well-being of humanity? Is it within the reach of the common man to aim directly at the well-being of humanity?

Krishnamurti: When we seek the well-being of one country at the expense of other countries, it leads to exploitation and imperialism. As long as we think exclusively of our own country, it is bound to create conflict and war.

When you ask whether it is within the reach of the common man to aim directly at the well-being of humanity, what do you mean by the common man? Are not you and I the common man? Are we different from the common man? What is there so uncommon about us? We are all ordinary human beings, are we not? Just because we possess clean clothes, wear shoes, or have a car, do you think we are different from others who have not these things? We are all ordinary—and if we really understand this, we can bring about a revolution. It is one of the faults of our present education that it makes us feel so exclusive, so much on a pedestal above the so-called man in the street.

23

Leaving School

I think it is a very rare thing, after leaving school, to find happiness in the latter part of one's life. When you leave here, you will be facing extraordinary problems, the problem of war, the problems of personal relationship, the problems as citizens, the problem of religion, and the constant conflict within society; and it seems to me that it would be a false education which did not prepare you to face these problems and bring about a true and happier world. Surely it is the function of education, especially in a school where you have the opportunity of creative expression, to help the students not to be caught in those social and environmental influences which will narrow their minds and therefore limit their outlook and their happiness; and it seems to me that those who are about to enter college should know for themselves the many problems that confront us all. It is very important, especially in the world that you are going to face, to have an extraordinarily clear intelligence, and that intelligence is not brought about by any outside influence, or through books. It comes, I think, when one is aware of these problems and is able to meet them, not in any personal or limited sense, not as an American, or a Hindu, or a Communist, but as a human being capable of bearing the responsibility of seeing the worth of things as they are and not interpreting them according to any particular ideology or pattern of thought.

Is it not important that education should prepare each one of us to understand and face our human problems, and not merely give us knowledge or technological training? Because, you see, life is not so very easy. You may have had a happy time, a creative time, a time in which you have ripened; but when you leave the school, things will begin to happen and enclose you; you will be limited, not only by personal relationships, but by social influences, by your own fears, and by the inevitable ambition to succeed.

I think it is a curse to be ambitious. Ambition is a form of self-interest, self-enclosure, and therefore it breeds mediocrity of mind. To live in a world that is full of ambition without being ambitious means, really, to love something for itself without seeking a reward, a result; and that is very difficult, because the whole world, all your friends, your relations, everyone is struggling to succeed, to fulfill, to become somebody. But to understand and be free of all this, and to do something which you really love—no matter what it is, or however lowly and unrecognized—*that*, I think, awakens the spirit of greatness which never seeks approbation, recompense, which does things for their own sake and therefore has the strength and the capacity not to be caught in the influence of mediocrity.

I think it is very important to see this while you are young because magazines, newspapers, television, and radio constantly emphasize the worship of success, thereby encouraging ambition and competitiveness which breed mediocrity of mind. When you are ambitious you are merely adjusting to a particular pattern of society, whether in America, Russia, or India, and therefore you are living on a very superficial level.

When you leave school and enter college, and later face the world, it seems to me that what is important is not to succumb, not to bow your heads to various influences, but to meet and understand these as they are and see their true significance and their worth, in a gentle spirit with great inward strength which will not create further discord in the world.

So, I think that a real school through its students should bring a blessing to the world. For the world needs a blessing, it is in a terrible state; and the blessing can come only when we as individuals are not seeking power, when we are not trying to fulfill our personal ambitions, but have a clear understanding of the vast problems with which we are confronted. This demands great intelligence, which means, really, a mind that does not think according to any particular pattern, but is free in itself and is therefore capable of seeing what is true and putting aside that which is false.

Index to Questions

2 *Fear Prevents Initiative*

How are we to gain the habit of fearlessness?..34

3 *Authority Destroys Intelligence*

How is one to be intelligent?...43
Everybody knows we are all going to die. Why are we afraid of
    death...43
How can we live happily?...44

4 *Understanding Freedom and Discipline*

Is it practicable for a man to free himself from all sense of fear
    and at the same time to stay with society?......................................49
What is God?...49
Can we be aware of our unconscious desires?.....................................50
Why are some people born in poor circumstances, while others
    are rich and well-to-do?..51
Is God a man or a woman, or something completely mysterious?.............52

5   *Learning How to Think*

How can we make our minds free when we live in a society
     full of tradition?..57
Since we have been brought up in a society based on fear,
     how is it possible for us to be free of fear?.............................58
What is real freedom, and how is one to acquire it?...................59

6   *Is There Such a Thing as Security?*

Why are we afraid, even though we know that God protects us?...............65
What is society?...66
Can you be free while living in this society?............................68
Why do people want to live in society when they can live alone?.............68
Since we are always related to one another, is it not true that
     we can never be absolutely free?..69
How can we be free when our parents depend on us in their old age?.......69
Would it be good on our part to allow our parents to starve?...................70

7   *Why Are You Ambitious?*

If somebody has an ambition to be an engineer, does it not mean
     that he is interested in engineering?......................................78
What is the easiest way of finding God?....................................78
Is God everywhere?...79
What is the real goal of life?..80
If I develop higher influences, will I eventually see the ultimate?...............82

8   *What Is Love?*

Why is there sorrow and misery in the world?............................87
If a man is starving and I feel I can be helpful to him, is
     this ambition or love?..89
Suppose I want to go home and the principal says no. If I
     disobey him, I will have to face the consequences. If I obey the
     principal, it will break my heart. What am I to do?....................90
Why should we not do *puja*?...90

9   *The Importance of Understanding Your Mind*

What should we ask God to give us?............................98
What is real greatness and how can I be great?............98
Is not love based on attraction?............................99
What is prayer? Has it any importance in daily life?............100

10   *On How to Listen*

Why do we feel a sense of pride when we succeed?............106
How can we be free of pride?............................107
How can a thing of beauty be a joy forever?............108
Why are the poor happy and the rich unhappy?............110
Though there is progress in different directions, why is
  there no brotherhood?............................111

12   *The Quality of Real Affection*

What is love in itself?............................120
What is religion?............................121
If somebody is unhappy and wants to be happy, is that
  ambition?............................123

13   *Understanding Is Not Memorizing*

Is beauty subjective or objective?............................128
Why do the strong suppress the weak?............................129
Is it true that scientific discoveries make our lives
  easier to live?............................130
What is death?............................130

14   *What Is Envy?*

Is truth relative or absolute?............................137
What is external awareness?............................139
What is real and eternal happiness?............................139
Why do people want things?............................140

15   *It Is Understanding That Is Creative, Not Memory*

Does intelligence build character?.................................147
Why does a man feel disturbed when another person looks
    at him intently?...149
Can we not cultivate understanding? When we constantly try to under-
    stand, does it not mean that we are practicing understanding?..........150
Is the power of understanding the same in all persons?.....................151

16   *Understanding the Significance of Words*

What is the purpose of creation?.................................157
What is karma?...158
Is there an element of fear in respect?.........................159

17   *Can the Mind Ever Find Peace?*

Why do we feel inferior before our superiors?...................164
Is it possible to have peace in our lives when at every moment
    we are struggling against our environment?.....................166
Why do we suffer? Why can we not be free of disease and death?.............167

18   *What Is Life All About?*

What is obedience? Should we obey an order even without
    understanding it?..173

19   *Living Intelligently*

Society is based upon our interdependence. The doctor has to
    depend on the farmer, and the farmer on the doctor. How then
    can a man be completely independent?.............................182
Why is truth unpalatable?..183
Up to now our teachers have been very certain and have taught
    us in the usual way, but after listening to what has been said here
    and after taking part in the discussions, they have become very
    uncertain. An intelligent student will know how to conduct
    himself under these circumstances; but what will those do who
    are not intelligent?...183

The farmer has to rely on the doctor for the cure of physical pain.
   Is this also a dependent relationship?................................185

20   *Being Educated Rightly*

I have everything to make me happy, while others have not.
   Why is this so?................................193
What is the way to get rid of the fear that we have?................................194
You said that if the parents really love their child they will not
   stop him from doing anything. But if the child does not want
   to be clean or eats something which is bad for his health,
   must we not stop him?................................196
Is it not important to have ideals in life?................................197
If we are small, how can we create a new world?................................198
What should be the system of education to make the
   child fearless?................................199
Is it possible to know the quality of gold without testing it in a
   special way? Similarly, can the capacity of each child be known
   without some sort of examination?................................199
Sir, what is your idea of a new world?................................200
How can we create anything new if we don't know what it
   is we want to create?................................200
Must the children take all these matters seriously? And if they do,
   will they ever be free to enjoy themselves?................................201

21   *Religion Really Is a Process of Education*

In your book on education you suggest that modern education
   is a complete failure. I would like you to explain this................................208
May I know why we should not fit into our parents' plans,
   since they want us to be good?................................209
You say that modern education is a failure. But if the politicians had not
   been educated, do you think they could have created a better
   world?................................209
If I want the right kind of education, do I need teachers?................................212
If all ambitions are stupid, then how can man progress?................................212
I have a friend who hates her parents because they have separated her
   from a person she loves. How can I help her?................................213
What is the definition of a student?................................214
You say that all idealists are hypocrites. Whom do you call an idealist?.....215

22 *To Discover the Truth of Things*

If all of us were educated rightly, would we be free of fear?......................219

You have said that to be ambitious is to be stupid and cruel. Is it then stupid and cruel to have the ambition to get the right kind of education?......................220

When one wants to find truth or peace, one becomes a *sannyasi*. So a *sannyasi* has simplicity?......................221

If we are educated in the right way we are free of fear, and if we are educated wrongly we are fearful. Is that true?......................221

If, as you say everyone is afraid, then no one is a saint or a hero. Are there no great men in this world?......................221

You said explanation is a bad thing. We have come here for explanation. Is that bad?......................221

What is your idea about the future of India?......................222

You say there are very few people in this world who are great. Then what are you?......................222

We read books out of inquisitiveness. When you were young were you not inquisitive?......................223

Should we not be concerned about the future?......................223

When we are young we are very playful and do not always know what is good for us. If a father advises his son for the good of the son, should not the son follow his father's advice?......................224

You said last time that the idealist is a hypocrite. If we want to construct a building, we must first have an idea of it. Similarly, must we not first have an ideal if we are to bring about a new world?......................224

By aiming at the well-being of our own country, do we not also aim at the well-being of humanity? Is it within the reach of the common man to aim directly at the well-being of humanity?......................225

Glossary

Bhagavad-Gita: Literally, "The Song of God," part of the Hindu epic Mahabharata.

Burning-ghat: In India, a *ghat* is a place, often with steps, where people descend to a river or lake, usually for bathing. Burning-*ghats* are reserved for cremation, so that the funeral party may have access to a body of water for purification and for disposal of ashes.

Coolie: Unskilled laborer.

Guru: A religious teacher.

Karma: The law of cause and effect operating in the moral world, as believed by the Hindus.

Koran: Sacred book of the Muslims.

Mantram: Words of divine power.

Nirvana: State of spiritual enlightenment or illumination. According to Buddhism, nirvana releases man from the cycle of birth, suffering, death, and all other forms of worldly bondage.

Puja: Hindu ritual worship.

Pundit: A scholar, especially versed in the Sanskrit lore of the Hindus.

Sadhu: A Hindu holy man or monk.

Sannyasi: A monk who has taken the final vows of renunciation according to Hindu rites.

Sari: A garment worn by Indian women.

Swami: A Hindu religious title.

Upanishads: Part of the ancient sacred Hindu texts called the Vedas.

Index

A

acquisition and clinging, 16, 29, 95
    disintegration and, 134–35
    envy and, 136–37
    fear and, 29, 30
    freedom from, 31, 172–73
    knowledge as, 180–81
    possession vs. love, 95–96
    property, desire for, 16, 95, 105
    reasons for, 140–41
    society based on, 126, 134–35
ambition, 3, 73–82, 194–95, 210, 212–13,
    220, 228–29
    class differences and, 52
    desire and the mind, 94–95
    fear and, 3, 74–75
    goal of life and, 80–81
    greatness and, 98–99, 221, 222–23
    of politicians, 209–10
    ridding oneself of, 10
    vocation vs., 78
arts and handicrafts, 12, 40–41, 71
attention
    concentration vs., 13

    cultivating, 15–16
    elimination of fear and, 14
    listening and, 104
    right thinking and, 14
austerity, 18. *See also* simplicity
authority, 32, 37, 38, 153, 164–66, 222–23
    code of behavior and, 38
    cooperative efforts and, 16–17
    curtailment of free mind and, 4, 153
    dependency and, 7–8
    destruction of intelligence and,
        37–44
    discipline and submission to, 4
    duty and, 154–55
    how it arises, 37–40, 119
    ideal as, 39
    obedience to, 173–75
    questioning, 42–43
    religion and, 159
    in a teacher, 3–4, 38, 41–42

B

beauty, 18–19, 105–6, 108–9,
    128–29

behavior
    authority and desire for safe conduct, 38–39, 40
    disinterested action, 14
    ideal, striving for, 39
    love as guidance for, 15
    modesty and courtesy, 11, 15, 18
    refinement in, 11, 105–6
    self-abandonment and, 18
    tradition and, 40
belief. *See* ideas
body, care of, 12–13
brotherhood, 111–12

C

change
    desire for permanence vs., 137–38
    revolutionary, 178–79, 190, 191–92, 208
character, 147–49
comparison or competition, 4, 5, 221
    acquisition and, 135
    greatness, 98–99, 221, 222–23
    happiness and, 193
    in the learning environment, 2–3, 4, 14, 191, 195, 197, 199–200
    love vs., 14
    memory vs. understanding and, 125–26
    mind as instrument of, 96–97
    See also envy
conditioning of the mind, 53–57, 103–4
contentment, 135–36, 158–59, 217–18, 222
cooperation and collaboration, 16–18, 154, 155
creation, 91, 181–82, 200–201
    education as opportunity for, 227
    free mind and, 30, 33
    purpose of, 157–58
    sacrifice and the artistic life, 71
    silence and, 14
    simple mind and, 219
    understanding and, 136, 144

what destroys it, 30, 33, 40–41, 91, 136, 153, 181–82

D

death, 9, 130–31, 168, 218
    fear of, 43–44, 167–68
dependency, 7–8, 26–27, 29, 30, 62, 85–86, 95, 141, 183, 185
desire, 50–51. *See also* ambition
deterioration (of human existence), 105, 106, 120
    duty, killing, and war, 155–56
    envy and, 133–37
    fear and, 153
    following and, 153, 155–56
    memory and, 143–44
discipline, 45–46, 205
    fear and, 119
    freedom and, 45–52
    loss of free mind and, 3
    submission to authority and, 4, 205–6
    teacher of student, 41–42
discontent, 14–15, 34, 162
    self-awareness and, 88–89
disintegration. *See* deterioration
duty, 154–55

E

education, 2–22
    authority and discipline in, 119–20
    as career preparation, 6, 23–24, 188
    competition or comparison (grades, exams), 2–3, 4, 14, 191, 195, 197, 199–200, 212
    failure of modern, 208, 209–10
    fear and, 26, 33, 189, 190–91, 197, 199, 219–20, 221
    function of, 22–27, 33–34, 76–77, 172, 187, 188, 210, 211, 217, 227–29
    intelligence and, 219–20, 227–28
    learning, what it is, 2–3
    leaving school, 227–29

love and, 4, 11, 14
as revolution, 2, 208
right education, 18, 33, 187–93,
    210–12, 214–15, 219–20, 221
schooling as amassing information,
    31
student, definition of, 214–15
as total development of a human
    being, 2, 4, 5, 9, 11, 14, 191–93
of unconscious (hidden) mind,
    19–22
understanding and, 178
understanding relationships and, 18
See also teachers
envy, 133–37, 143, 147, 153
experience, 21, 114, 116, 180–81
understanding vs., 144, 145

F
family, 66–67. See also parents
fate, 51–52
fear, 25–27, 118–19
ambition and, 3, 74–75
attention and, 14
avoidance of, and conforming,
    58–59
behavior and, 118–19
comparison or competition as
    breeding, 2–3, 4, 14
confronting as way of eliminating,
    58, 194, 219
consequences of, 26, 120, 153
creation inhibited by, 41, 180–82
of death, 43–44
dependency and, 7–8, 26–27,
    29, 30
education and, 2, 26, 33, 189,
    190–91, 197, 219–20, 221
freedom vs., 26, 31, 33, 34–35,
    57–58, 175, 190
God as protector and, 65–66
imitation and, 33
initiative prevented by, 26–27,
    29–35

intelligence and, 25, 43, 206, 219
inward, 29
knowledge and, 113
love as banishing, 15–16
mistaken as love, 84–87
need for security and, 61–65
origins of, 73
outward, manifestations of, 29
pervasiveness of, 189
religion and, 203–8
respect and, 159–60
sensitivity inhibited by, 41
society and, 49, 58–59
solitude and eliminating, 10
teaching, approach to, 3–5
tradition and, 26, 29–30, 33, 54,
    57–58
understanding banished by, 27
universality of, 25–26
feeling, 19
self-awareness of, 85–86
following. See imitation
freedom, 130
acquisition vs., 31
alienation from society and, 57
conditioning vs., 56–57
discipline vs., 45–52
education and, 26, 33, 199
fear vs., 26, 31, 33, 34–35, 57–58,
    175, 190
imitation vs., 31, 56–57, 173
intelligence and, 3, 34, 42, 59, 130,
    183, 198, 218
revolt and, 57–58
sensitivity and, 48
tradition vs., 31, 57–58
understanding and, 127

G
God, 49–50, 154
asking of, 98
as belief, 87
experience of, 116, 122
female or male nature of, 52

God (*continued*)
  finding, 78–79, 98, 114, 172, 173, 204, 210
  omnipresence of, 79–80
  as protector, 65–66, 122
  religion and, 179, 171–72, 203–8
  revolt in order to find, 208
  tradition and perception of, 52
  understanding and, 137
gurus
  authority of, 32, 38
  following, 32, 50, 172, 179
  illusions vs. truth and, 50

H
habit, 31, 34–35, 119, 154
happiness
  beauty and, 108–10
  comparison and, 193
  as contentment, 135–36
  following and lack of, 46
  as lack of conflict, 139–40, 153, 162
  in later life, 227
  life choices and, 47
  living with, 44
  poverty vs. wealth and, 110–11
  pursuit of, 123, 153
  state of, recognizing, 44, 193–94
  unconsciousness and, 44
hate, 213–14

I
ideals, 39, 86, 117, 127, 146, 149, 195, 197–98, 224
  comparison and, 96–97, 126, 127
  idealists as hypocrites, 195, 215, 224
  self-acceptance vs., 99
ideas (beliefs), 17, 63, 200, 207
  deterioration and, 170
  as deterrent to inquiry, 14
  older people and, 80, 93
  propaganda and, 104
  psychological security and, 61–65
  reading and, 223

  religious, 121–22, 203–8
  truth vs., 16
imitation (following), 30, 32, 153, 178, 179, 195–96
  awareness of, 32
  character and, 148–49
  conditioning as, 54–55
  duty, cooperation, and obedience, 155–56, 173–75
  freedom from, 31
  ideals and, 198
  initiative destroyed by, 30, 126
  memory and, 144
  religion and, 159
  in society, leader and led, 126
  of superiors, 164–66
  youth and, 55
initiative, 27, 91, 172, 217
  conditioning as destroying, 56
  fear as destroying, 26–27, 29–35, 70, 120
  imitation (following) as destroying, 30, 126, 153
integration (oneness of self), 133
intelligence, 5–6, 179–80
  authority and destroying, 37–44
  character and, 147–49
  education and, 24–25, 219–20, 227–28
  fear and, 25, 43, 206, 219
  freedom and, 3, 34, 42, 43, 46–47, 49, 59, 130, 183, 218
  growth and, 198–99
  lack of exploitation and, 129–30
  living intelligently, 177–82, 184–85
  self-awareness and, 149
  tradition and inhibition of, 46, 47
  vocation and, 77–78

K
karma, 51–52, 158–59
killing, 155–56
knowledge, 13, 14, 113–16, 180, 217
  love with, 115

scientific progress and, 111–12, 130,
144–45, 212–13
teaching and, 145
total development vs. narrow, 14
tradition as, 40, 113
understanding vs., 144, 145

L

learning
acquisition of information and, 2,
113–16, 217
atmosphere and environment that
cultivates, 7, 8
attentive mind vs. concentration,
13–14
competition, comparison, as deterrent, 2–3, 4, 14
conditioning as, 53–57
coercion as deterrent, 2
discontent as motivation for, 14–15,
34
eagerness for cultivating, 7
how to think, 53–57
imitation vs., 9
natural curiosity and, 7
security of student and, 7, 8, 14
solitude and, 9, 10
student-teacher relationship and,
7–9
life
complexity of, as increasing with
age, 217–19
destruction and misery in, 74,
87–89
difficulty of, 228
future vs. now, 222, 223–24
happy, 44
listening to, 145
living intelligently, 177–82
memory and knowledge as
destructive factors, 145–46
ocean metaphor for, 188
purpose of, 80–81, 157–58
relationships and, 182–83

state of the world, 187–89, 192–93,
209–10, 222
as suffering, 123, 131, 169, 218
what it is, 131, 154, 169–73
youth stage of, 201, 217
listening, 103–5, 107, 127
loneliness, 65, 204
love, 10–12, 10–11, 83–91, 177
ambition vs., 89–90
attraction and, 99–100
behavior and, 11, 15
brotherhood and, 111–12
comparison absent from, 4, 14, 97
creation and, 191–92
death and, 132
dependency and fear vs., 84–87, 95,
118
disinterested action and, 14, 118,
121
duty and following vs., 156
in educational environment, 7, 11,
90
expressing through manual work
or creativity, 12
expressing through the senses, 12
intrinsic, 120–21
knowledge and, 115
mind's destruction of, 94
parental, 83–84, 86
peace and, 161, 163, 164
possession and, 95–96, 99–100
quality of real affection, 117–20
refinement and, 105, 106
respect and, 160
self-abandonment and, 18
sensitivity and, 10
sex and sexuality and, 11–12
understanding and, 182

M

marriage, 64
meditation, 91
solitude and cultivation of
sensitivity, 9

memory and memorizing, 6, 109–10, 125–27, 143–47

mind
attention vs. concentration, 13–14
beauty as state of simplicity, 18
closed, 46, 223
conditioning of, 53–57
developing to be capable of confronting life, 3
disciplined, 3–4, 46
discontent and growth, 14–15, 34, 162
ego (me, mine) and, 96, 106–8, 114, 115, 116, 137, 180–81, 182
experience, effect of, 21
fear as crippling to, 30
free, need for, 33, 50
free, what it is, 30–31
innocence vs. calculation, 18
as instrument of comparison, 96–97
limitations of, 14, 140, 170, 223
listening and, 103–4, 107
peace, finding, and, 161–64
right thinking, 14
search for God or truth and, 10
self-awareness of, 3, 93–101
simple (vs. complex), 218–19
state of inquiry and learning, 9, 10
still mind, 98, 152
thoughtlessness, 119, 159, 174
timeless and beyond permanence, 138, 182
tradition and memory, effect of, 14
unconscious vs. conscious, 19–22, 39–40
understanding and freeing, 143
unity with body, 12–13
wheel of dissatisfaction and gratification and, 14–15

modesty and courtesy, 11, 15, 18
morality, 9, 118

N

nationalism, 171, 222, 225

P

parents
conditioning of child by, 53–57, 198
conflict with, 69–71, 213–14
goals of education and, 6, 192
love and, 83–84, 86, 196–97
obedience to, 173–75, 213
plans for child, 209, 224
psychological and real property inheritance from, 16
questioning, 42–43
right education and, 6–7, 16, 192, 196–97
security and, 63, 64
teacher's relationship with, 7, 16

peace, 161–64, 166–67, 177, 221
poverty, 51–52, 66, 110–11, 158–59, 187–88
power and domination, 129–30
prayer, 100–101
pride, 106–8
progress, 111–12

R

refinement, 11, 105–6
relationships
freedom and, 69
parent-child, 6–7, 16, 42–43, 53–57, 63, 64, 69–71, 83–84, 86, 173–75, 192, 196–97, 198, 209, 213–14, 224
society as, 182–83
student-teacher, 7–9, 183–85, 199

religion, 121–22, 177
acceptance and contentment and, 135, 158–59, 217–18 (*see also* karma)
acquisition and, 136, 172–73
education and, 206–8, 210
fear as basis of, 203–8
imitation and, 159
love and, 10–11
prayer, 100–101
puja, performance of, 90–91, 121

questioning, 32
ritualism, 55, 90–91, 121
true vs. dogma, 10, 170, 171–72
understanding vs., 137
respect, 8–9, 159–60
respectability, 148
revolution
    authority opposing, 198
    freedom and, 57–58
    and new world created, 16, 190,
        191–92, 207–8
    as radical transformation of the
        mind, 2, 16, 17
    social and economic, 1, 4
    society of equals, creating, 4

S

scientific progress, 111–12, 130, 144–45,
    212–13
security, 8, 61–71, 73
    attention and, 14
    authority and pursuit of, 39–40
    child's need for, 7
    conditioning and, 64
    cultivating, 8–9
    fear as creating need for, 61–62, 122
    freeing oneself from, 65
    knowledge for, 115
    psychological (inward), 62–64, 73
    respect and, 8
self-awareness, 93–101, 112, 139
    barriers and, 151–52
    of desire, 51
    development of a good mind
        and, 3
    of imitation, 32
    intelligence and, 149
    questioning and introspection, 81
    response to others and, 149–50
    and solitude, daily practice of, 10
    teachers and, 184
    truth, finding, and, 82
    understanding and, 151
self-reliance, 159, 172

sensitivity, 9, 48, 177
    accepting teacher's suggestions
        and, 9
    dependency and crushing of, 8
    discipline and destruction of, 48,
        119
    fear and inhibition of, 41, 48
    freedom and, 48
    love and, 10
    morality and, 9
    perception of beauty and,
        128–29
    refinement and, 105
    self-absorption vs., 150
    solitude and cultivating, 9, 10
    youth and, 163–64
sex and sexuality, 11–12
silence, 104–5
simplicity, 18, 146–47, 218–19, 221
society
    acquisitive, 126, 134–35
    ambitions and conflict, 73–74,
        76
    conditioning by, 53–57
    duty, killing, and war, 155–56, 177
    fear and, 49
    freedom and, 68, 69
    future of, 222, 223–24
    inequality in, 165–66
    leader and led as a basis of, 126
    nationalism, 171, 222, 225
    need for, 68–69
    new, creating, 166–67, 197–98,
        200, 207
    obedience to, 173–75
    old sacrifice the young, 156
    peace and, 162, 166–67
    poverty in, 51–52, 158–59, 165–66
    relationships and, 182–83
    socio-economic classes, 77,
        149–50
    what it is, 49, 66–68, 166
solitude, 9
    daily practice of, 10

suffering
    acquisition as cause of, 96
    deadening of, 218
    discontent and, 14
    fear of, 44
    life as, 123
    reason for, 87–89, 167–68
    running from, 123

T

teachers and teaching
    authority and, 3, 7–8, 37–44, 90,
        119–20, 184, 198
    comparing and evaluating stu-
        dents, 5–6, 14, 191, 199–200, 212
    discipline of student, 41–42, 119
    education, purpose of, 25, 27
    fear and, 26, 178, 199, 212
    and function vs. status, 5
    goal of, 10, 74, 77, 78, 196
    as imparting a sense of freedom, 3
    as job, 192, 212
    love and, 11, 14, 15
    as noble profession, 18
    parents, relationship with, 6–7, 16
    respect, cultivating, 8–9
    right education and, 211–12
    self-awareness and, 192, 199
    student-teacher relationship and,
        7–9, 183–85, 199
    subject matter for students, 5
    thinking limited by memory, 145
tradition, 14
    as authority for behavior, 40
    class in society and, 47–48
    as consequence of fear, 26, 54
    as deterrent to inquiry, 14
    freedom vs., 31, 46, 47, 49, 57–58
    as habit-forming mechanism, 31
    in India, 31–32, 53, 54
    initiative prevented by, 29–30

intelligence inhibited by, 46
    knowledge as, 113
truth, 16
    cooperation and, 17
    the divine and, 50
    education and, 210
    freedom and, 140
    free mind and, 50
    imitation as blocking, 153
    relative or absolute, 137–38
    seeking, 46, 82, 170, 172, 217–19,
        222–23
    self-awareness and, 138
    simplicity and, 221
    symbol (words) as shadow of, 154
    understanding and, 126
    as unpalatable, 183
    youth and importance of, 156–57

U

unconscious mind, 19–22, 39–40
    listening and, 127
understanding, 125–27, 136, 151, 158, 178,
    219
    barriers to, 151–52
    cultivating, 150
    love and, 182
    memory vs., 143–47
    self-awareness and, 151
    youth and, 167

V

vocation, 76–77, 177
    ambition vs., 78

W

women
    education for, 24
    tradition, conditioning, and, 56
    treatment of, 32
words, power of, 147, 153–57, 163

About the Author

One of the great spiritual philosophers of our time, Jiddu Krishnamurti was born in 1895 in Andhra Pradesh, India, to middle-class Brahmin parents. When he was fourteen, members of the Theosophical Society, a Western spiritual movement that combined Eastern and Western religious traditions, found him walking on a beach and became convinced they had found the new World Teacher. Subsequently, theosophist Annie Besant adopted him and raised him in England. By the 1920s he was attracting worldwide press attention and audiences of thousands. In 1929, after an awakening and much self-questioning, he abandoned the Theosophical Society and set out on his own, teaching a philosophy bound by no caste, nationality, religion, or tradition.

"Truth is a pathless land." Man cannot come to it through any organization, through any creed, through any dogma, priest, or ritual, not through any philosophic knowledge or psychological technique. He has to find it through the

mirror of relationship, through the understanding of the contents of his own mind...*

For more than sixty years, Krishnamurti traveled the world speaking to millions. His talks and writings have been preserved in over seventy books. He died in 1986 in Ojai, California.

---

* from "The Core of the Teachings," J. Krishnamurti.

Addresses of Krishnamurti Foundations

Krishnamurti Foundation of America
P.O. Box 1560
Ojai, California 93024-1560
U.S.A.
Email: kfa@kfa.org

Krishnamurti Foundation India
64-65 Greenways Road
Vasanta Vihar
Chennai
India   600 028
Email: kfihq@vsnl.com

Krishnamurti Foundation Trust Ltd.
Brockwood Park, Bramdean
Hampshire SO24 0LQ
U.K.
Email: info@brockwood.org.uk

Made in the USA
San Bernardino, CA
16 March 2017